"I Hereby Resign"

"I Hereby Resign"

Job Transitioning: How Individuals Properly Prepare, Resign and Move to the Competition, and How Companies Best Manage That Process

Steven L. Manchel, Esq.

Washington DC

Printed in the United States of America

Library of Congress Control Number: 2019944370
ISBN 978-1-7330408-4-6 paperback (alk. paper)
ISBN 978-1-7330408-5-3 hardcover (alk. paper)

 An imprint of New Academia Publishing

 4401-A Connecticut Ave., NW #236 - Washington DC 20008
info@newacademia.com - www.newacademia.com

To my wife Sharon, my greatest transition ever…

Contents

Introduction

It is the moment you have been waiting for with great anticipation and real dread. It is the moment when you finally get to step out of the shadows. At precisely 2:00 p.m. on Friday, you knock on the manager's door and say, "Have a second?" As you approach the desk, you notice the manager's eyes drop to the letter in your left hand. The manager watches intensely as you, her direct report, sink down into the chair across from the desk and take a moment to adjust your seat. Deep breath, and then those magic words are spoken: "I am resigning, effective immediately."

Every year, millions of people voluntarily leave the company for which they work to join a direct competitor. Additionally, over the course of a typical working career, a person is likely to change jobs upwards of ten times, and of those moves most will involve going to the competition. Millions more every year consider, perhaps explore, the notion of quitting their jobs in order to join a competitor. All such undertakings, even if the decision ultimately is made not to leave, bring great legal and litigation and business risks that can result in large damage awards, injunction orders, and general business disruption and turmoil.

"But," and I hear it all the time, "why should I worry about any of this stuff, let alone being sued, since I do not have an employment agreement or a non-compete clause?" Sorry, but there is still a need to worry. In brief, the absence of an employment agreement, or a non-competition or non-solicitation or non-recruitment clause, does not mean you are in the clear. On the contrary, in my experience, the most costly litigation has concerned unlawful *pre-resignation* misconduct. Consequently, the how-to steps set forth in this book address how to act *before* you say "I quit," namely, what actions you may properly take before you resign to move to a competing company, all of which have nothing to do with whether you have a contract with your current employer.

I also hear regularly about how many people leave to join the competition, never get sued, and never have any business problems at Next Company. Empirically, that is correct; all sorts of folks have changed jobs without ever incurring any legal or business problems. It is equally true, however, that there are large numbers of people who end up in costly litigation over a lateral move and who suffer serious business setbacks. Just think about it: If there are no such risks, what do you think has been keeping me in business for the last thirty years? This book thus presents a very simple question: Do you want to be one of the "unlucky" ones who get sued and/or have their business plans materially disrupted? Put another way, are you willing to take a chance of leaving the wrong way *and* being caught? If you are not so willing, I have a relatively short book for you to read.

For almost thirty years, I have been advising individuals on how to properly resign and move to the competition, and how companies best manage that process. As a result, what's in this book is new. Historically, the hiring process has typically been structured into just three segments: attracting, interviewing, and onboarding. Attracting is the effort companies generally undertake to make people want to join. Interviewing, of course, is the process by which potential candidates are winnowed down to the hire. Onboarding, which is classically broken down into two subparts (the proverbial "Day One" activities and, later, company socialization), has traditionally been the last defined step of the hiring paradigm. However, I have come to understand that this tripartite approach to hiring is too narrow and has unnecessarily created many costly and avoidable lawsuits and business headaches.

In a word, until now, the discipline of moving to and hiring from the competition was missing one very important step: *Transitioning*.

Transitioning, which is the sole focus of this book, covers the time between when you decide you are interested in perhaps leaving your company, to when you knock on your manager's door to resign. What can you properly do to prepare? What should you do and what can you do before resigning to ensure not only smooth Transitioning, but also to make certain that you do not leave in a way that creates disruptive and costly litigation? What can and can't you discuss during the hiring process? When should you resign? What should you say when you quit? To whom should you resign if your boss is out that day? How should you draft your letter of resignation? Can you go secretly into the office the night before resigning and take your personal stuff? What information can you properly keep? Can you, before resigning, tell revenue sources and co-workers that you will be leaving? What if you are a manager or senior executive yourself? Should you determine, before resigning, who will come with you? *How can you make sure that you prepare and resign and leave the right way?*

Who should read this book? The target audience is anyone involved in the process of moving to and recruiting from the competition: The individual who is thinking about leaving, headhunters, business owners, executives, supervisors who recruit, in-house corporate lawyers dealing with the legal risks of lateral hiring, and owners of companies. Why should anyone read this book? Because here are some unalterable truths about moving to or hiring from the competition: Industries are shrinking, in terms of competition; high-ranking executives are valuable; people and revenue are portable; many candidates have employment agreements; companies do not like to lose revenue or personnel to a competitor; and leaving the wrong way will result in litigation that is costly and damaging.

Allow me to give you a sense of what shapes my views. I have handled, directly and indirectly, conservatively, over 2,000 "lateral" transitions—defined as an employee or group of employees moving from one business to a direct competitor—over the course of practicing law for the past thirty years. In so doing, I have represented CEOs, doctors, fund managers, headhunting firms, and hundreds of securities representatives and insurance agents. I have also done work in almost every industry imaginable, from retail to food to sports to pharmaceuticals to ambulances (true) and soap and aftermarket machine parts. I have even represented lawyers moving to a competing law firm. Every week, still, my firm advises multiple individuals who are leaving where they work to join a competitor, and we also take care of the companies that are doing the hiring. I have litigated, arbitrated, mediated, and managed employee movement disputes all over the country and internationally.

At the heart of this book, therefore, is how to manage both the law and the *psychology* of Transitioning. Remember, the central premise addressed here is the notion of someone who decides to leave a company and join a direct competitor. Good Transitioning requires a disciplined focus on the governing law, as well as a real appreciation for the feelings, emotions, and optics, and often the fear and anger, that are natural byproducts of Transitioning. Thus, what I seek to impart is how individuals who are Transitioning, and how companies doing the hiring, understand not only the general legal requirements imposed on Transitioning, but also the overall temperament of a well-run departure process. Look, any good attorney can read an employment agreement or a non-competition clause or handle a piece of litigation. But how do you manage the risk and scope of litigation before there is a lawsuit, before you have even resigned? Moving to another company, especially to a competing company, is akin to a divorce. Is it going to be a nasty divorce, or one that, under the circumstances, is manageable?

How did I get involved in writing a book about this topic? Well, approximately twelve years ago, I read with interest an article written by a then-relatively new Harvard Business School assistant professor named Boris Groysberg. The article concerned research conducted by Professor Groysberg on approximately forty job transitions. The focus of the exercise was to memorialize observations made by this gifted teacher about pre-departure actions that did, or did not, lead to post-resignation business success. Since not everyone succeeds at the next company, the research provided important business insights into how to better position yourself, before resigning, to do well at the next firm. The paper was written thoughtfully, supported with validated data, and filled with sound business observations.

While perhaps good for business, the pre-departure activities described in the article raised the potential for great legal risk.

I have always been intrigued by the fundamental tension between what are unquestionably good business practices—success being defined by top notch performance at the next company—and the legal roadblocks or speed bumps placed upon such pre-resignation activity by the law. Indeed, I have spent my entire career working at marrying these sometimes seemingly polar opposite forces. While reading the article, I found myself once again experiencing those proverbial crosswinds, so I emailed Professor Groysberg and suggested that we meet to discuss what appeared, at least on the surface, to be a conflict between the actions taken by some of the people about whom he wrote, and my litigation experience.

What followed from our first meeting has been, in this order: One of the most meaningful friendships I have in my life; the pleasure of helping to draft the case study you are about to read; teaching that case study for now over ten years, and before more than 1,000 Harvard Business students; and the resultant marked sharpening of my overall professional skillset. During these last ten-plus years, Professor Groysberg and I have spent countless hours discussing, sometimes arguing, about what a hiring business wants to see happen quickly and the legal brakes placed on that process. Our relationship is thus ultimately a reflection of this book overall: A collaboration between legal and business forces with the fundamental goal of making Transitioning successful. Also, without question, I received back from the students I lectured at least as much if not more than I had hoped to give them. Besides being bright and motivated, the Harvard Business School students I met came from so many different cultures and communities and socio-economic perspectives that the Harvard Business School classroom became, to me, a microcosm of what our entire world should strive to be: A gathering of good, smart people with unique and valid viewpoints, from different cultures, who nevertheless civilly and respectfully share their values and thoughts in ways that better us all.

Teaching at the Harvard Business School also reflects in a concrete way the validation, if you will, of the message I have been delivering now for many, many years. Think about it: I am a lawyer teaching in a business school, not at a law school. My choice of academic forum was purposeful. My overarching professional opinion is that the successful blending of law and business delivers the greatest value to the client. Again, any decent lawyer can read a non-competition agreement, or come to understand the law governing departures and hiring. Similarly, any good businessperson can be trained to be a solid recruiter. But the lawyer who gives sound legal advice wrapped in an entrepreneurial business vision is the lawyer you want helping. Consequently, this book will also greatly help you choose your legal counsel.

Let's return briefly to an important point worth repeating: Any time someone leaves to join a competitor, there is a significant risk that a lawsuit will follow. That given comes from a number of very real, very serious laws and rights and obligations that are implicated by any such move, be they contracts, trade secrets, confidential information, or the host of general legal duties employees owe to their current employers before resigning. But there is another immutable truth: Nothing, including the safeguards set forth in this book, can stop a lawsuit from being filed. So, you ask legitimately, why continue reading? Because it is possible, very possible, to greatly mitigate your exposure, both legal and business.

How to use this book is also important. On the surface, this is a book mostly for individuals. The goal is to break job Transitioning down into discreet, understandable, and easy-to-follow steps that, in turn, help shield the person who is Transitioning from great legal risk. Consequently, Part One of this book focuses directly on the person who is leaving. The process is separated by chapters into a series of practical points: Chapter 1 sets out what I call the "Dos and Don'ts" of leaving a company; Chapter 2 addresses "The Art of Resigning," including how to draft a proper letter of resignation; and Chapter 3, entitled "I am Don Jenkins," helps readers assess their true ability to leave a company and to understand what assistance, such as what type of legal help, they need to obtain.

Part Two of the book focuses on how a hiring company can and should develop a program to manage Transitioning effectively. For those skeptics out there who claim that one book cannot speak to both individuals and companies, I have this to say: Keep up that attitude and continue to watch the lawsuits fly. Transitioning by definition involves *both* the individual being recruited and the company doing the recruiting, so they *have* to be in sync. In other words, the individual can do everything perfectly right, but if the company is not equally well prepared, the company could ruin it all. Conversely, if the company knows precisely how a recruit should transition, but does not effectively impart that vision, what good is the knowledge? Also, an individual Transitioning should be able to tell if the hiring company is a good Transitioning partner. It takes two to dance the recruiting dance, and the only way for both partners to be coordinated is for everyone involved to understand how proper Transitioning occurs on both sides of the proverbial manager's desk.

My legal training and client obligations require that I highlight here a few additional important threshold matters.

What you are about to read will provide a solid understanding and appreciation for how Transitioning should work, how Transitioning impacts companies, and how an individual Transitioning from one job to join the other side should behave. That being said, I am vigilant about protecting the privilege and confidentiality of communications with my clients. Consequently, I cannot relate in this book, verbatim, what advice I have rendered or communications I have exchanged, nor can I identify (directly or even by detailed description) the clients to which or to whom I have provided advice. Thus, for example, the book is filled with anecdotal stories that highlight the particular points being made; however, because of the constraints under which I write, those stories are in large measure created from a number of different-yet-similar-in-nature experiences, as opposed to a single event. To be clear, the events described are real, but I have merged facts and separate happenings and taken literary freedoms in order to make the point and be certain that no one reading this book will be able to tell who actually was involved in any given situation.

Also, when addressing the questions and challenges presented by Transitioning, no one can rely solely on this or any other single writing. Why? Because, as you will see, a great number of varied and varying factors attach to and affect every transition. What should be done in any particular Transitioning is always driven by the unique facts of that situation, and by the applicable law, all of which change state by state, country by country, industry by industry, and even within a profession (think doctors and nurses). As such, it would be irresponsible of you the reader, and of me the author, to treat what follows as everything possibly applicable to every potential departure. While I believe strongly that the information contained in the following chapters is important and that it will, alone, greatly enhance the quality of how each Transitioning proceeds, it will not and cannot provide verbatim directives workable in every instance. For all these reasons, the book is designed to give readers a meaningful, practical and clear view of how best to begin to manage the ever-growing phenomenon of leaving one business to join the competition. It will also, frankly, help companies and individuals choose and then assess the capabilities, cost, and value of their legal counsel. There is one more benefit: Good recruiting and good recruiting practices beget more good recruits.

Now, I invite you to enter my "class." Over the course of our time together, I will take you to those parts of the following case study that, for me, raise particularly thorny—and oftentimes overlooked—issues that arise when an important employee leaves for the competition. The answers to those questions are spread out over this book. But please don't cheat by looking for them before you read the study, as struggle is always the best teacher. Indeed, in over ten years of teaching this case study to approximately one hundred sixty students per year, at a business school that is at least as well respected (and deservedly so) as any in the world, precious few have spotted the clues discussed below. Frankly, that is one of the main reasons I decided to write this book!

Okay. It's now 2:00 on Friday.

Knock, knock....

Don Jenkins: Between Opportunities[1]

"Another day, another dollar," Don Jenkins thought as he put the last box of papers into the trunk of his new BMW 325. "Too bad they aren't Canadian dollars," Don chuckled to himself as he reflected on the recent U.S./Canadian currency exchange rate. It was Friday afternoon and Don was in a cheerful mood. He had just slipped his resignation letter (Exhibit 1) under his boss's door at Smolthouse Planners, the world's leading event planning firm. After more than five years as a lead planner at Smolthouse, Don had accepted a managing directorship at the competing boutique planner, Bud Fox Productions.

Two Months Prior

Two months prior, Don had a brief conversation with Cecilia Benner, a managing director (MD) at Bud Fox, while attending a professional development event put on by the local chapter of Meeting Professionals International (MPI). Cecilia and Don knew each other from business school at Stanford and had both ended up pursuing careers in the event planning industry after graduation. Don won a coveted position at the prestigious firm Smolthouse, while Cecilia signed on with Bud Fox, hoping that she would be able to move up more quickly through the ranks because of the

1. Copyright 2019 by the President and Fellows of Harvard College. Harvard Business School Case Study. This case was prepared by Boris Groysberg, Geoff Marietta and Steven L. Manchel under the direction of Boris Groysberg for class discussion rather than to illustrate either effective or ineffective handling of an administrative situation. Reprinted by permission of Harvard Business School.

firm's smaller size. Cecilia proved to be right and was promoted from lead planner to MD after four years. Meanwhile, Don continued as a lead planner at Smolthouse hoping that he, too, would be promoted to MD. But, Don was growing impatient and had begun to consider his options when he saw Cecilia at the MPI session.

"So, how is the MD position treating you?" Don asked Cecilia during a coffee break.

"It's a lot of work, but I love all the responsibility. I oversee five lead planners and have anywhere from four to six events to keep track of every week. It's exhausting, but so rewarding when you can solve that last minute...well, you know how it is. So, how is Smolthouse going these days?" Cecilia asked.

Don didn't want to speak poorly of his company, especially at an MPI event, but hearing Cecilia go on about her work as an MD made him feel jealous and frustrated that he hadn't been promoted despite the exceptional reviews he received every year. "Well, you know, work is work," Don replied.

Cecilia looked around the room cautiously and drew close to Don. "Hey," she started, "you didn't hear it from me, but one of the MD's at Bud Fox is leaving for a VP job at...well...another firm. So, we are going to be looking for someone to fill that position and I think that management is looking for someone from the outside, you know, for some fresh ideas. Anyway, if you're interested, I can pass it along. What do you think?"

Don paused, "Uh, yeah sure. I mean, yes, I am interested. Yes, thanks Cecilia, let them know that I would love the opportunity to interview. It will all be confidential, right?"

"Yes, of course, Don. You can trust me."

Smolthouse Planners

Smolthouse, a subsidiary of the large media conglomerate View Corp., had offices in 63 locations around the world and planned events and meetings that ran the gamut from birthday parties for five year olds with clowns and donkey rides to esteemed, Hollywood awards banquets that cost millions of dollars. The firm prided itself in its ability to "plan any event, for anyone, anywhere." Smolthouse also had a reputation in the industry for being extremely competitive, some would even say cutthroat, for top clients. In fact, Don had been told during his first interview at Smolthouse that he was expected to create his own book of clients, and more than 75% of his compensation was based on the revenue those clients brought into the firm. Don still remembers what the interviewer had told him. "At Smolthouse, we believe that the harder you fight to sign a client, the more responsibility you take in delivering his or her dream event."

After three grueling interviews that lasted a total of twelve hours Don received word that he had been offered a position at Smolthouse. He accepted the offer immediately. After taking the offer, Don was surprised at the informality of the rest of the hiring process. He received a few congratulatory phone calls from MDs and a letter that spelled out the offer for lead planner. Don received a base pay of $40,000 and a bonus of 30% of total event planner fee revenues for all events he led. Smolthouse didn't even have Don sign a non-compete.

The first few months at Smolthouse were tough for Don. There was no training or orientation session. Don was simply shown his desk, and given a laptop, network password, and a stack of papers with prospective clients' contact information. Don then began calling. Seven-hundred calls and ten days later, Don had yet to sign on a client. From the beginning, Don had vowed not to take the advice that all his co-workers gave him—to pick the low-hanging fruit first—F&F, short for Friends and Family. But, after the second straight week of rejection, Don grew desperate and thought that calling a few of his more well-off friends from business school couldn't hurt any. He started with his good friend Jack, whose family Don knew owned several car dealerships in the area. As luck would have it, Jack's Uncle Benny had three daughters and a son, ages, 11, 13 and twins, 15 and wanted to plan a big birthday party for the twins, Elizabeth and Joshua's, upcoming 16th birthdays.

Sweet Sixteen Birthdays

Unbeknownst to him at the time of signing Benny on as his first client, Don had stumbled onto the dramatically growing market segment of sweet sixteen birthday parties. The sixteenth birthday had always been a big event for parents and their teenage children alike. In most parts of the U.S. and Canada, it marked the age in which a person could get a driver's license and was an important childhood highlight for many adolescents. The sixteenth birthday also had been popularized by the 1984 film, *Sixteen Candles*, starring Molly Ringwald, and songs by Hillary Duff, Billy Idol, Chuck Berry, and even Neil Sedaka.

Don worked hard to make the 16th birthday party for the twins go off without a hitch. The $140,000 event had over 400 guests in attendance, a five course Tex-Mex themed dinner, and a live performance by Elizabeth and Joshua's favorite band. Benny was so impressed by the event that he told all of his friends about Don and Smolthouse Planners. Within a few months, Don had four clients wanting sweet sixteen birthday parties for their children, each costing over $90,000.

At Smolthouse, lead planners and MDs began to seek out Don for his knowledge on extravagant children's birthday parties. In the middle of the third year, Smolthouse asked Don to sit on a subcommittee to help determine its one, three, and five-year strategic plans. Don contributed immensely to the process, helping Smolthouse design its strategy for pursing the burgeoning birthday event market in the U.S. By the fourth year, Don had planned over 55 events and developed a list of over 70 past and prospective clients. He had also been able to develop a strong four person team of assistant planners, each specializing in such areas as food, music, decorations, and venues.

A few MDs had even begun giving Don other events to plan, including anniversaries, weddings, and a few corporate retreats. However, while Don was quite successful in developing his own franchise during this time, things were not going well for Smolthouse as a whole. To Don, the troubles began when his MD of four years, Lindsay McNeil, left for a senior position with a corporate client. Lindsay had served as Don's mentor since his arrival at Smolthouse and he was quite disappointed to see her go. Don thought he might be a good candidate to take Lindsay's place, but Smolthouse management decided to promote Sarah Martin, a lead planner with 12 years of experience, to fill Lindsay's spot as MD. Then Smolthouse missed the earnings target set by its parent, View Corp. After the failure to hit the set benchmarks, executives from View Corp. made a visit to Smolthouse and delivered a speech about "actively managing costs" and "seeking stable revenue streams." Don had heard that bonuses were going to be cut to 20% of planning revenues and for the first time ever Don received questions about his submitted expense reports. An issue had also arisen within his team. The assistant planner responsible for food, who Don had handpicked for the job, had asked for a raise. But Don couldn't give an answer to the team member because all compensation issues now had to be handled and approved by executives at View Corp.

During his fifth annual review, Don had expected to be promoted to MD. His planner revenues had grown over 25% a year and Smolthouse had earned over $2 million from the events Don had planned. Furthermore, over the past year Don had been able to secure several corporate clients, which provided more stable revenues than individual high net worth clients. At the review, Sarah Martin praised Don for his hard work and exceptional performance. However, she still wanted Don to get more experience in planning different types of events before being promoted to the MD position.

The Bud Fox Offer

Several days after talking to Cecilia at the MPI event, Don received a call from the head of human resources at Bud Fox. "Wow," Don thought, "that didn't take long." The HR head wanted to know if Don could come in for an interview in the next week for an MD position that had just recently opened. Don checked his schedule and set a time for the interview.

The interview at Bud Fox was fairly informal. There were a few MDs, the head of HR, and a VP in the interview. Don knew nearly everyone; the professional event planner community was fairly small. The VP began the interview.

"Don, we're quite familiar with your outstanding work at Smolthouse. We just have a few questions for you and then we'd love to spend the rest of the time answering any questions you might have for us. First, if we offered you the MD position here at Bud Fox, would you bring any of your clients with you? How willing would they be to make the move?"

Don was prepared for the directness of the first question. After a brief pause, Don responded. "My clients chose me, not Smolthouse.

I am sure that they would continue to demand my services. In fact, I was just speaking yesterday with one of my clients who happens to be the CEO of a large multinational manufacturing company. He was asking me when I was going to leave and hang out my own shingle because he hated dealing with the rest of the people at Smolthouse."

Several questions later, the interview seemed to be over. The VP then asked Don if he had any questions. Don thought that a discussion about compensation would come up later in the process, but now seemed like a good time so he decided to broach the subject at the interview. The head of HR didn't seem surprised at all and said that Bud Fox would be willing to give Don a generous market rate for the MD position. Don asked a few more questions and the interview ended.

The next week Don received a call from the head of HR at Bud Fox.

Don felt excited about this unexpected opportunity. The position offered a big increase in compensation and responsibility. Plus, Don would be working alongside his old business school classmate, Cecilia. The only drawback seemed to be trying to keep the offer secret from his boss at Smolthouse. Over the next several weeks Don negotiated back and forth on his compensation package. After Bud Fox met most of his requests, Don formally accepted the offer.

The Weeks Before Resigning

Don's last few weeks at Smolthouse were busy. A new client had called with an urgent request to plan a big corporate event for the Friday Don had intended to resign. After several tense discussions with the client, Don was able to convince her to postpone the event for one week, giving him more time to plan and the ability to hit the ground running at Bud Fox. He also had to make preparations for his transition to Bud Fox. Don updated his client list, sent it to his personal email address, and printed out a few hard copies to take with him. Don also had to make sure that his clients were aware of his move to Bud Fox, so he prepared a short letter with his new contact information (see **Exhibit 2** for the letter template).

Things went more smoothly in the last few days that Don expected and it appeared that word had not leaked out about his move. "My event planning skills have come in hand in resigning from Smolthouse," Don thought. To top off his last week, Sarah Martin had left early on Friday for her son's birthday party. "Perfect," Don thought, "no one will know anything until Monday."

Exhibit 1: Don Jenkins' Resignation Letter

January 5, 2007

Dear Sarah:

First, I'd like to say that I have really enjoyed my time here at Smolthouse. I've learned a lot from everyone, especially you, about how to plan the perfect event and make clients happy. However, at this point I am moving on to a new challenge. As of today, I am resigning from my lead planner position at Smolthouse to accept a managing director position at Bud Fox Productions.

My resignation has nothing to do with the way I have been treated at Smolthouse. Everyone here has always been extremely nice and professional to me throughout my five years as a lead planner. It really meant a lot to me when you helped put together the party for my birthday and I will always remember the flowers you sent after my grandmother passed away. It has been a great time here at Smolthouse and I will miss you all.

That being said, I'd also like to say that I am worried about the direction that Smolthouse is heading. It seems that View Corp. has a different idea of the future of event planning. I worked really hard on the strategy subcommittee to try to put Smolthouse in the right direction, but all my work is being squandered. If Smolthouse continues to give in to the bureaucratic processes and policies implemented by View Corp., it will drive many of its talented planners to join competitors. Honestly, I think Smolthouse is headed straight for an iceberg and if things don't change soon it'll end up just like the Titanic, only this time I don't think they'll be any survivors.

But, all in all, I've enjoyed my time at Smolthouse. I've learned a lot and hope to remain friends with many of the people I have met here. Good luck in the future and keep in touch.

Sincerely,

Don P. Jenkins

Exhibit 2: Don Jenkins' Client Update Letter Template

Dear (insert client name here):

I wanted to thank you for selecting me as your event planner for (insert event here) and take the opportunity to give you an update about a change in my life.

I will now be working for Bud Fox Productions as a Managing Director. I would not have made the move unless I believed that my service to you would be dramatically enhanced. Bud Fox provides an outstanding platform for me to design and execute any event you have in mind. So, please continue to keep me in mind as you think about future special events.

Below is my new contact information at Bud Fox.

Sincerely,

Don P. Jenkins

(insert new address here)
(insert new phone number here)
(insert new email here)

So ends the case study. Before moving on, before having the benefit of my insights and experience, take on the following challenge: See if you can articulate what Don and the hiring company did right and wrong. Take a moment, if you will, to put yourself in Don's shoes, and in the spot of the company recruiters, and see how you would have acted—what you would have said and done—without yet having read what you are about to read. You see, most people who change jobs have many of Don Jenkins' tendencies... if left to their own devices. In other words, not coached, Don is the norm, not the exception. However, I am certain that, by the time you finish this relatively short book, your views and actions will be quite different.

PART ONE

HOW INDIVIDUALS PROPERLY TRANSITION

For those of you on the corporate hiring side, you will see in Part Two of this book how the lessons in Part One serve as the anchor to any good Transitioning Program. Consequently, put aside for the moment your "company hat" and step into the shoes of the recruit. For you folks who are considering a job move, take good notes on what comes next. Yes, there will be a quiz!

Chapter 1

The "Dos And Don'ts" Of Transitioning

Unless you are properly prepared before you quit, you will create great legal exposure and risk to yourself. To help you move safely and properly to the competition, I want to focus on the time between when you start to think about another job, and when you join Next Company. As a threshold matter, please pay careful attention to how I define the relevant timeframe: Transitioning covers the time from when an individual first thinks he might leave, until Day One at New Company.

I need to give a small lecture.

For the moment, forget about whether you have an employment agreement. Let me say that again: Forget about whether there is an employment agreement. When it comes to what behavior or actions can and cannot occur before you resign, with few exceptions not relevant here, it does not, repeat, does not, matter whether you have a contract with your current employer. Understandably, many people believe that, if they are not contractually prohibited from becoming an employee of a competitor (a so-called "non-competition" clause), and are not barred by an employment agreement from attempting to take revenue sources to the competition (a "non-solicitation" clause), or are a manager not subject to a non-recruitment clause, then the process of joining the competition is free of restraint and legal risk. Not so. While the absence of an existing employment agreement might make life easier once you resign, it has very little to do with what you may and may not properly do before resigning. Thus, it is critical to know the pre-departure, pre-resigning, rules of the road.

There are four Rules that govern Transitioning. Having now

helped hire, directly and indirectly, more recruits in more states than I can possibly count or recall, I fully appreciate that there are also nuanced, important differences from state to state, from country to country, from industry to industry, and from profession to profession. I also firmly believe that such varied legal and business factors must always be accounted for, which is why I regularly affiliate with lawyers across the United States who assist me in recruiting matters. However, what I have learned, and what I am about to impart to you, is that if you can come to understand what I call the four "Dos and Don'ts," then you (and the hiring company) have already substantially reduced legal and business risk.

What are the four Rules?

1. Don't Pre-Solicit Revenue Sources

Rule Number One, really is Rule Number One: You should not pre-solicit revenue sources (for those of you who are managers, this Rule is equally applicable to subordinates). First, please pay attention to the word *solicit*. In most circumstances, *solicit* means to communicate for the purpose of getting your audience to do something, to cause someone to act. The classic example of a solicitation is calling a client for the purpose of getting them to switch their business from Old Company to New Company. Be forewarned: In most states, it does not matter who initiates the contact; a solicitation can occur even if it is the client who calls you and first says, "Let's you and I discuss how maybe I will go with you to New Company." If your response to that hypothetical incoming call is to pitch the client about Next Company, that will almost certainly be deemed a "solicitation." Be forewarned further, even offering a choice—"if I were to join Company A, Company B, or Company C, would you come with me"?—almost always constitutes a wrongful pre-departure "solicitation." It also makes no difference, typically, whether the pitch is made orally or in writing. Thus, the only safe course before you resign is to stay away from speaking in any way about Next Company with your revenue sources (or subordinates).

Second, note the breadth of the potential audience not to be solicited: "revenue sources." I did not say "clients." Often, people get hung up on technicalities (says the lawyer with an almost straight face). Arguments break out over whether someone is a "client," or a "close friend" or "just a center of influence." I'm always hearing things from recruiters like, "Why can't my candidate tell just this one guy about where he is going? The guy he wants to tell was the Best Man in his wedding." People: I don't care who the guy is, or what labels are used to describe the guy, or that the guy is the candidate's "absolute best friend in the whole world, just like a brother." When asked about whether someone can be an exception to this Rule, I respond with just two straightforward questions: Is the person whom we are currently discussing (the "Best Man") a source of revenue, directly or indirectly, for the company you are about to leave? Do you intend and hope to divert the "Best Man's" business (or employment) to your new company? If the answer is yes (and it is always yes), then you may not speak to the revenue source about Next Company until you have resigned and joined Next Company.

Did Don follow the Rule? This is actually the first test to see how well you read the case study. Before moving on, do yourself a favor and go back and re-read the study to see if you can spot the answer. Fair warning: In more than ten years of asking this same initial question to Harvard Business School students, precious few have ever figured out the answer. Thus, if you claim to know now, before turning to the next paragraph, how Don did, well, let's just say I am skeptical.

Don did not honor the "No Pre-Solicitation" Rule. Did you spot what Don did? If so, again, you would be among just a handful of people who figured that out. For those of you who are being honest, go back and take a look at Don's letter to his clients. It was the second letter attached to the case study. Did you happen to see what's wrong with that letter? Better put, did you pick up what's *missing* from that letter? I will tell you what is missing: Where is the date? Who writes a letter without a date? I will tell you that, too: Someone who does not want a record of when it was sent. But why would someone want to hide the date on which a client letter was sent? I will tell you that as well: Because they knew it was being sent before it was proper to send. Listen up folks: If someone makes a hire from one of my clients, and the (now) former employee sends out an undated letter to revenue sources, I will eventually get my hands on that letter and I will sue both the person who resigned and the company for which they went to work. *A candidate cannot pre-solicit revenue sources.*

With each Rule comes a story.

I am hired by companies all over the country, and sometimes internationally, to make sure that their Transitioning recruits leave in accordance with these (general) Rules. In every single instance, we discuss Rule Number One, the "Do Not Pre-Solicit" Rule. Inevitably, we hear back the typical "I get it, I understand, I will comply" type of remarks. Sometimes, such as in the story that follows, as my oldest son would say, "LOL."

Once, on the very night after walking someone that day through the Dos and Don'ts, including explaining in detail Rule Number One, I get a call from one of my closest friends who lives in Atlanta. He says to me, "I just got a call from my financial advisor. He told me that he was leaving his company to go to another company and that he wanted to get all of my transition paperwork completed before he resigned. Isn't that the kind of stuff you do?"

That's right: My client, after I told him that he absolutely could not solicit anyone before he resigned, *pre-solicited someone I knew personally.*

So early the next day, I called the recruit and said, "Hey, just wanted to follow up on our conversation. I heard a rumor that you were already reaching out to clients. Don't."

Unwilling to take the bait, or to confess, the recruit said, in response, "No. I listened to you. I'm good."

"You good, you really good?" I asked. (The most memorable cross-examinations occur when you let the witness dive deep into the lie.)

"Yep. All good. Haven't spoken to anyone."

"Then why did my close friend Ben Harrison call me last night?"

"What did you just say?" he bleats out. "You broke up."

I can hear him starting to free fall on the other end of the line.

"Ben Harrison. He and I grew up together in Vermont. He now lives in Atlanta. We've been friends since second grade. I think you know him. In fact, *I think you two spoke last night.*"

Rest assured, the balance of our talk was, shall we say, memorable.

I'm telling you straight: People who pre-solicit revenue sources (or subordinates) will get caught, and the hiring company and the candidate will suffer.

Let me also be clear about something discussed already in part: I fully appreciate the inherent tension created by this Rule. What better way to start at a new company than by lining up your clients, revenue sources, centers of influence, or key personnel in advance to ensure that they will be doing business with you on your first day on the new job? Right? That way you can impress your new employer and get a great jump start on hitting those bonus targets! The problem, though, is that you are trying to get ahead for the next company while still working for your current company. In almost every state in which I have handled recruits, the law provides that, if you are a Transitioning employee, you may not compete with your current company while still working for that company, and that the act of even seeking clients, revenue, or personnel commitment for the next company is deemed an unlawful act of competition. So don't. If the sources you value really are loyal, they will follow.

That last point is important and worth repeating: People who do not pre-solicit their revenue sources or pre-recruit their subordinates are not only acting in accordance with the law, they are demonstrating the strength of their relationships. If Don really needs a secret head start, just how much faith does he actually have that his clients will follow him? Is he so afraid they won't come with him to Bud Fox that he has to cheat? As for Bud Fox, how good can it feel about hiring someone who has to lie and break the law in order to be "successful" at the company?

Please pause for a moment to also reflect on another related point: By far, and I mean by far, the largest litigation and arbitration awards and settlements with which I have been involved arose out of scenarios where employees pre-solicited revenue sources or pre-recruited subordinates. If you think lawsuits over violations of employment and non-competition agreements generate the biggest litigation headaches, think again. Rule Number One is therefore really Rule Number One for a reason. Let me also be clear about something else: You might, just might, get away with pre-soliciting or pre-recruiting, but when that luck runs out, the resulting litigation—just one lawsuit—could wipe you out.

2. Books And Records

In the context of Transitioning, why have a Rule about documents
and information? Because what we are addressing here is the moving and hiring of experienced personnel. Consequently, by definition, you are someone who has accumulated a lot of material that
you believe, for all sorts of reasons (some valid, some not so valid),
is mission-critical to your future success. Shoe designers want to
keep their design portfolios. Engineers love their drawings. Chefs
want their recipes. For those who directly serve clients, the coveted information ranges from names and addresses to, in the case of
the financial services industry, birth dates, Social Security numbers,
and account numbers. The point is that every person thinking about
Transitioning to a competitor believes they must keep something
in order to better their chances of success at Next Company. Then
there is the personal stuff you want, and I've seen it all: trophies,
pictures, antiques, TV sets, dental records (swear), rugs…it is end-
less. What are you allowed to take without creating great legal risk
for both you and the hiring company?

The answer (generally) has two parts: one practical and one legal.

Legally, in almost every state in which I have helped a company
hire from the competition, before resigning you may take nothing.
In certain industries, in certain states, under certain circumstances,
there are valid arguments to be made that a recruit, before resigning, may take, for example, basic contact information; *i.e.*, name,
address, telephone number and e-mail address. Note that I am being purposefully vague here: The taking of any information, even
contact information, raises very serious legal issues that vary state
by state and even by industry norms; in some situations, the practices of the company from which you are resigning also have an
impact on this question. The issue is complicated further, typically, by the presence of what is called a "confidentiality clause" in
an employment agreement. In essence, a confidentiality clause is a
contract term that spells out what an employee has agreed already,
and in writing no less, is confidential information belonging to the
company. Trust me, taking information—any information—brings
with it great exposure and risk.

Practically speaking, there is another reason why a Transitioning employee should leave things in place: The easiest way to spot that someone is planning to resign is to see something important missing from the office. And by "something" missing, I don't necessarily mean client data or financial information. Take the suddenly absent picture of the family: A beautiful portrait that has been sitting on the left corner of your credenza, behind your desk, for the last seven years. Where did it go? Why is it not in its usual spot? When your manager walks in and sees the open space on the credenza, she will think either you are having family trouble, or you are getting ready to quit. What other reason would there be to remove that picture? Reframing, perhaps? Right. I hope you get the picture (admittedly terrible pun). Besides what the law requires, *if you want to resign on your own timetable, do not remove even personal items in advance of resigning.*

Let's, as they say, double-click on that last comment about personal items: Removing personal items is, as noted, a classic tipoff that someone is leaving. Also, there is almost always no such thing, in the context of Transitioning, as personal items. Look, I get the fact that, for example, the tax returns you keep in your work cabinet are yours. However, in almost every state in which I have helped people Transitioning, you still should not take out even the tax returns until after resigning. Also, I won't debate with clients (or the opposition) about what is personal and what is not personal. If you take material from my clients in the dark of night, you will hear from me, and then we will discuss what belongs to you in a whole other framework.

The first cousin to the Rule about not removing items from an office before resigning is how to deal with electronic, or computer-based, information. Let's start this discussion by looking first at the moment after you quit. Spotting improper pre-departure computer activity is incredibly easy. Rest assured that any company worth its salt will immediately have an IT person all over your computer and, if relevant, your cell phone. Did you e-mail any information from your work computer to your home e-mail address? Don't. Was a thumb drive attached to the server in order to transfer files and information? Don't. (Even if you subsequently destroy the thumb drive, which should never be done, I can still tell the make and model of the thumb drive used, the dates on which it was used, and every file accessed.) Instead of a thumb drive, did you insert a floppy disc? Ready for the answer? Don't. Are you looking at files or data that you would not normally review? All such activity suggests to the now-former company that wrongful pre-departure conduct has occurred. Consequently, it is critical that people getting ready to compete against their current company stay away from accessing or using information stored on the company server.

A further note about destruction and deletion of business information. Don't. Before you hand in the computer the company bought for you, unless you have been so instructed, do not have it wiped clean. As a threshold matter, it is almost always the case that, even though you think you have destroyed all of the information, it is still largely recoverable by a computer forensics expert. More important, deleting or destroying business information is itself an unlawful act in most states. Know also that the legal consequences of taking such acts of "spoliation" are severe. So please do not delete or destroy anything having to do with your current employer or regarding Transitioning to Next Company.

Perhaps more than any other aspect of leaving a company, questions about the pre-resignation handling of information must be addressed on a case-by-case basis by a lawyer before you quit. It is, admittedly, once again a delicate balance between the law of each state and your personal business goals. You simply cannot shy away from addressing the topic, and no one, really, can fully handle questions about Books and Records on their own. Yes, there will be legal costs, but think of all the wonderful success that will follow and spend just a drop of that success up front on sound legal advice. By the way, absent something unusual, the advice should take less than an hour.

Here is a great "taking stuff" story because it shows that candidates don't always follow this Rule, and that nothing good happens when a recruit violates Rule Number Two.

I get a call one day from a manager who is hiring an individual with whom I am already working. As is sometimes the case, especially in smaller cities with fewer high-end corporate buildings, this individual, when he resigns is literally moving from one floor to another floor in the same building. In other words, his current company and his soon-to-be-next company share the same parking lot, elevators, cafeteria, *etc*. As my youngest son would say, "Awkward!"

The hiring manager starts the telephone call with me by saying that he "needs my advice."

"Sure," I say, "what's going on?"

"Well, I am looking out my office window, which faces a nice little park across the street, and I think I see our guy running around the park, screaming and gathering up papers that are flying all over the place."

Given what I have seen and heard in this business, I am unfazed. I say, calmly, "Let me call and see what's going on."

I finally reach the employee on his cell and I repeat what the manager told me.

After a brief pause, I get the confession. "Sorry, I did not follow your advice. I removed and boxed up a bunch of documents that I just could not do without. When I was putting the last of the boxes in the trunk of my car, which was parked just outside my building, the tops of the boxes blew off and the wind took the papers across the street and shot them all over the park. Yes, that was me chasing after them."

The park, I thought wryly as I listened, that is visible to both the current company and the soon-to-be-former company. Sure enough, in less than a week after the move, the former company sued and, in the lawsuit, described in great detail the "flying" client papers that covered the park outside its windows.

Go back and see how Don handled the Books and Records Rule. What you will see is similar to what Don did with respect to Rule One: He acted poorly, but not atypically. This is an important point: What Don did was wrong, and it created great legal risk for both Don and Bud Fox; however, in my experience, what he did was not *unusual*. Why? Because without proper counseling, everyone's instinct—yours and the hiring company's—is to hoard and keep documents and information. Look also at the things Don did in the weeks before resigning: He "updated his client list and sent it to his personal email" (which quite possibly could be the easiest "bad act" for a company to spot); and he "printed out a few hard copies of his client list" (printing, especially using printers with counters, is not only wrong, it is a classic sign of an employee getting ready to leave). This is precisely the type of pre-resignation conduct that creates great risk for you and the hiring company, and which therefore you must avoid. Let me put it in the clearest of "legal" terms: *Don't take stuff!*

3.   Don't Change Your Work Habits

Rule Number Three also has two parts: one legal and one practical. Let's begin with the practical.

Every day you have people watching you. Not like Big Brother, but simply people with whom you interact regularly, and who are therefore tied into the rhythm of your day. If you always come in at precisely nine in the morning, and then suddenly start arriving at 7:00 am, co-workers will notice. If you talk on a cell phone with the office door closed, as opposed to using the office telephone with the door open, the administrative assistant will notice. If your attendance at meetings falls off, or productivity drops, the boss will notice. If you now have two cell phones instead of one, other employees will notice. If your new briefcase is twice the size of the old briefcase (so you can, against my advice, spirit out documents), people in the office will notice. If you are suddenly much more vocal, much more aggressive, about challenging what displeases you at your current company, the CFO will notice. *When you change your behavior, it sends out a signal that you are leaving.* The practical piece, then, of this Rule is to be very, very sensitive to not changing your "normal" business behavior. If you and the hiring company want to keep the departure schedule, then you need to maintain your work habits.

The legal part of Rule Three is equally straightforward. The law in almost every state and country in which I have worked with recruits requires the same pre-departure work behavior. Specifically, until the moment you resign, your duty—in legal terms it is often called a "Duty of Loyalty"—is to your current employer, and not to your soon-to-be-new employer. For example, if, pre-resignation, a terrific new revenue source arrives on the scene, your legal duty is to bring that revenue into the current firm. Oftentimes, however, your instinct is to do otherwise; choosing, understandably, to keep the revenue source at bay until you have made your move. "What's wrong with just putting them off for a little bit, right? I'm leaving in one week, what's the harm? If I can push things out a few days then I immediately get a great new revenue source at the next company and, still better, that revenue source never had any relationship with the former company. So smart!" (Remember how Don convinced a potential new client to postpone the event for a week?) I use a word for such unlawful conduct: "Warehousing." The law, almost everywhere I have run up against this issue, has a fancier phrase: "Usurping a Corporate Opportunity." Either way, we get to the same result. It is almost always illegal to take for yourself, or to push off for the next employer, a business opportunity that presents itself while you are still working for the company you are about to leave. Bottom line: Absent something unusual as you are getting ready to leave, if faced with opportunities that you are unsure how to handle, act as if you are not going and then decide.

Who among you spotted Don's failure to maintain his work habits? Go try and see what happened, and then read on.

First, what did the case study say about how things were going at Smolthouse when Don decided to leave? Remember? "Don had heard that bonuses were going to be cut to 20 percent of planning revenue for the first time ever." Smolthouse also had "missed the earnings target set by its parent" company. Then, "for the first time ever Don received questions about submitted expense reports." In the midst of all that economic downturn and heightened focus on expenses, what did Don decide to do? (Go read again how the case study began.) At the very moment the company was announcing reduced bonuses and facing challenging economic times and watching all expenses, what did Don choose to drive to work? Yes, a *new* BMW. Who buys a new, expensive car at a time when the company is reducing employee compensation and focusing on how money is being spent? I will tell you (I will always tell you): The person who just got a signing bonus from their next company!

Every recruit needs to understand that they must be very sensitive about maintaining their work habits each and every day until they resign.

Sometimes, people take this Rule too literally, and do not actually think about what they are doing.

One day, I had a call scheduled with a Transitioning candidate to talk about next steps. The discussion was set to occur about a week after we had gone through the Dos and Don'ts. As such, the recruit already had been lectured on the Rules, including of course the "Don't Change Your Work Habits Rule." The hire assured me that, when we spoke, it would be "normal and natural" for him to be "out of his office." Remember, leaving your office when you would not typically be away from your desk sends a signal. All good, right? We have a well-trained candidate and a spot-on attorney who gave great legal advice. What could go wrong? As my wife would say, "Hah."

A few seconds after the call began, the recruit's voice suddenly drops without notice to a whisper. Seconds later, it rises back to a typical speaking level. Ten seconds or so passes, and his voice lowers again to barely audible, only to be followed, again, by substantially increased volume. This rather strange sound pattern continued for a bit until finally I interrupted and asked him if there was something wrong with our connection. He said "No," and asked me why I had asked. I said, "Because the volume, your voice, keeps fading in and out."

In response, I am told, "That's because, in order to do this call, I had to leave my office, like you said."

"Okay," I replied, now even more confused.

"So, I left my office and went to the main conference room, which is in the middle of the floor. That's where I'm calling you from now. Every time someone walks by, I have to lower my voice."

"Let me get this straight," I say. "Your approach to my instruction that we speak at a time when it would be normal for you to be out of your office, was to leave your office, go to a conference room in the middle of the *whole* firm, which I assume is all glassed in, and then sit there on a cell phone talking to me while people walk by? *That was your solution?*"

What I got back was a timid, "Yes?"

Not a good move. Adhering to the "Don't Change Your Work Habits" Rule requires you to think about your pattern of behavior: What is the message you are sending because of how you are acting? Talking on a cell phone in the central conference room while your boss walks back and forth is not the way to maintain your work habits!

4. Don't Lie

Rule Number Four sounds the simplest, but I think it is the hardest. First, why does this Rule even exist?

Almost everywhere, with a few (important) exceptions, the law allows you, in legalese, to "prepare to compete." Thus, for example, most departing employees can lease new space, or create business cards, or undergo training on the next company's systems, all before resigning. These actions can typically also be done in secret; in other words, the current company usually has no right to know about such preparations. While the examples of lawful preparation behavior are numerous and seemingly varied, for an experienced lawyer (which, as discussed in Chapter 3, you should consult) they all share a unifying link: The Transitioning activity is what I call "internal." Put another way, no appropriate pre-departure activity involves you taking so-called "competitive actions," such as reaching out to revenue sources in order to pitch the new company (Rule Number One). In most instances, if you follow Rules One, Two, and Three, you will be able to lawfully and privately prepare to leave, and no one will discover your plans.

Sometimes, though, a candidate gets what I call "flushed out." Perhaps management spotted a change in behavior, or a drop in productivity. I've had other instances where the hire was seen at a restaurant often used for recruiting lunches or dinner (or coffee); or, worse yet, someone spotted the recruit coming out of a competitor's workplace. It is also not unusual for a manager, who is managing in a struggling work environment such as Smolthouse in the case study, to jostle the highest-ranking employee whom she sees at risk of leaving. What all of this leads to is the classic "manager pops her head unannounced into the office doorway and, in a strained but casual voice, says 'I hear you're leaving'" moment.

Hence the need for Rule Four: If that happens, don't lie. If so confronted by the manager, you must be prepared to fight your first instinct, which is to make something specific up so the manager goes away; *e.g.*, "I am not even thinking about going anywhere, I love this place!" Instead, in most cases, push back at "30,000 feet." Typically, stay general; in fact, stay as general as the manager. Say things such as, "I don't know how these rumors get started." "I am doing the best I can." "You know better than anyone that things are a bit rough around here." Using such general phraseology, in almost every instance, pushes the inquirer off. It also stops you from lying. The reason such an approach works typically is because the manager does not really know that you are leaving; she is just fishing around. You should practice out loud responding to this scenario.

Here is a wonderful "don't lie" story.

I am at the gym one day working out on the treadmill when my cell phone rings. The caller is a candidate who is scheduled to resign the next day.

"You cannot believe what just happened," he whispers into the phone.

"Where are you and what happened?" I ask.

"I am in my office, I know not to call you from my office, but I had to."

"What happened?" I ask again.

"The postman just delivered to my office, instead of my house, the client mailing I am going to be sending out when I join [Next Company]."

Now, let me pause my account of the conversation so you can fully appreciate the moment. This is a candidate who has not yet quit. He has prepared a client announcement mailing that is going to be sent out to his clients (numbering in the hundreds if not more than a thousand) *after* he joins New Company. The mailing is thus incredibly voluminous. Boxes and boxes of envelopes. Because it was prepared for Next Company, not his current employer, the mailing, naturally, was supposed to have been delivered to his home. Instead, the announcement—for the new company—was now stacked in six large brown boxes in his soon-to-be-old office. Remember: *No lying!* Back to our talk....

"What should I do if my manager comes in and sees all the boxes?" he asks.

"Tell him the truth," I said. "Tell him it's a mailing you are going to send to your clients."

The manager of course came in, saw the boxes, and asked what they were for, and the candidate looked him straight in the eye and, truthfully, said, "It's a mailing for my clients."

And the manager left, satisfied!

"Don't Lie" is thus both a short and important Rule to get across. Some of the worst, most litigious, most expensive recruiting cases I have handled involved senior management who believed they had been lied to by the resigning employee. Again, for the most part, you have the right to prepare to compete in secret. It is an important right, and it must be safeguarded. However, nothing is worth the loss of your reputation or integrity. Therefore, if you believe, really believe, that the company knows you are leaving, be honest and say it's true. Yes, the hiring timetable will be disrupted, but a good Transitioning Program, discussed in Part Two of this book, will be prepared for such an event. So, Don't Lie!

These four Rules—the Dos and Don'ts of pre-departure behavior—generally represent the basics, the substantive foundation, if you will, of how you should prepare and behave while Transitioning. Understanding and following these four Rules (tailored of course to the particular applicable law and unique circumstances of each move) greatly protects all participants from legal and business risk and ensures that individuals behave as they should on the way out the door.

Chapter 2

The Art Of Resigning

Only people who are really, really ticked off quit on the spur of the moment. People who are well prepared plan their resignation. Artfully resigning involves four distinct but equal and related pieces: Choosing the date on which to resign; choosing the person to whom you will resign; drafting a proper letter of resignation; and knowing what to say, and not say, when you resign. Sounds simple, right? Sure.

1. Resignations Occur On Friday

Absent something concerning a particular departure that convinces me to the contrary, I believe candidates should always resign on a Friday. Using my own almost thirty years of experience as a marker, I would venture to say that substantially all of the Transitioning in which I have been involved included resigning on a Friday. Take a guess why it should happen on a Friday. I bet you guessed wrong: It's in large part out of courtesy; yes, courtesy. Resignations, especially group resignations, are disruptive and emotionally charged. People's feelings are hurt, businesses are scrambling to assess damages and next steps, and other employees are watching the fallout. The best resignations, therefore, are done respectfully, succinctly (which I will come to in a moment), and at a time when calmness and reflection have a chance of resurfacing—namely, the afternoon before a weekend.

Even if you choose the correct day on which to resign, you can still choose the wrong moment to resign. I think Don chose poorly. But you say, "Hey! Don chose a Friday and you said Friday was the right day!" Yes, Don correctly chose to resign on a Friday; however, do you remember what was happening, what he knew was happening, on that particular Friday? Specifically, do you recall what his boss was doing at the moment he chose to slip the letter under her door? In fact, wasn't his supervisor's absence the reason Don chose to resign at just that time? Don's timing alone, just the timing of the resignation, will result at best in Don having created a lifelong enemy. At worst, what he did to his manager, if she carries enough weight at the company, will itself result in litigation. That's because Don put his boss in an untenable position: Either she abandons her child's birthday party in order to attend to the business mess caused by Don's departure, or she forgoes her job responsibilities to be with her son.

The art of resigning thus begins with an appreciation of when, and when not, to resign. Bottom line: Don't be a Don Jenkins when you go to resign. Choose the right day and the right moment.

2.   Choosing The Right Person

The next step is to choose the correct person to whom to resign. In some industries, and in some businesses, that is not as simple as it sounds. For example, in the securities industry, in order for a registered representative to electronically transfer their license, they typically have to resign to what is known as a designated "Principal." In many instances, however, that Principal is not the representative's day-to-day boss. In other industries, or in smaller companies, daily operations are managed, in essence, by committee, thereby making it difficult to choose "the one boss" among the group. Many recruits we handle are the manager, so to whom do they resign? The unifying logic, for me, is, absent something unusual, to always resign to the person whom you believe is the first line supervisor impacting your employment; *i.e.*, the person who typically directs (or reviews) your daily work.

But again, alas, the choice should not be made the way Don chose. Actually, if you recall, Don did not choose to resign to anyone. Those of you who read the case study carefully will remember that Don "just slipped his resignation letter under his boss's door[.]" Not a good move. We don't allow recruits to slip letters under a door and run. But to be perfectly clear, unless there is a contract provision that governs how you must resign in order for the resignation to be effective—and I have seen such clauses, so beware—or an industry licensing requirement, you typically do not have a legal obligation to resign in person. Nevertheless, we insist that all recruits always resign to someone (resigning over the telephone may also be appropriate when, for example, you work remotely from your boss). Why? Because intentionally sneaking out of the office on a Friday afternoon when your supervisor is at her son's birthday party defeats the two fundamental purposes of resigning: The hiring company needs a definitive record of the termination moment (so there is no argument about when you may properly begin work at New Company), and setting a courteous, professional tone upon departing.

Also, a word to the wise: Don't convince yourself that you "have" to resign to the president of the company (unless the president is your actual boss) because of how important you are, or some type of thinking to that effect. Unless there is a substantive reason not to do so, you need to resign *just* to your immediate supervisor. Multiple resignations never lead to good things.

Here's an instructive "I'm a big deal" story.

This particular candidate worked for a very large public company that still had the founder at its helm. During our discussion about how to resign, he tells me that he is, "such good friends," and "so close" with the founder that he "just has to resign" to the founder in person, instead of resigning (as instructed) to his direct supervisor. To make things even "better," the recruit has decided, in his infinite wisdom, to resign to the company chairman late on the Wednesday afternoon before Thanksgiving Day.

I tell him not to do it. I tell him he may very well be important, but the chairman is not his actual boss. I tell him also that the date, the timing, is all wrong. "On the Wednesday afternoon before Thanksgiving," I say, "all he wants to do is get home to his family. If you really are important, and you resign, you run a great risk of at best interrupting his holiday. So please don't."

The candidate, of course, does not take my advice (at least I got a story out of it).

I wait all that Wednesday to hear how the resignation went.

Late that night, I get a call from the recruit.

"I couldn't do it," he says.

"Couldn't do what?" I respond with remarkable legal brilliance.

"I couldn't tell him I was resigning when he asked me why I wanted to see him."

"So, let me get this straight," I said (yes, I really like that phrase). "You made the founder of a public company stay late on the day before Thanksgiving, when all he wanted to do was be at home with his family and, then, when he asked why you wanted to see him, you lied?"

Not a good move.

Fast-forward a week. It's now about ten days after Thanksgiving, and the guy resigns to his direct supervisor. Within approximately two hours of the resignation, maybe less, I am on the phone with the general counsel, the top lawyer of the now-former company. He knows me because we've had cases in the past against each other. The message was short and to the point and, I might add, quite effective: "I just want you to know, Steve, that on this one, I have an unlimited litigation budget." Click.

Bottom line: Absent something unusual, resign to the most direct supervisor you have and forget about how supposedly "important" you are to the proverbial "president."

3. The Letter Of Resignation

A letter of resignation serves three very significant purposes. First, it marks the moment of separation; a bright line event for the candidate, the hiring company, and the company the recruit is leaving. (Also, as my law partners, who are classically trained in employment law, can tell you, all sorts of rights—and obligations—contractual, statutory, and at common law are triggered upon resigning.) Trust me, on more than one occasion I have seen disputes over whether or when a recruit has resigned. It is not something you want to leave to chance. When you are ready to resign, go see your supervisor with a letter in hand and deliver that correspondence to formally establish the moment of termination (if the resignation needs to be by telephone, then the letter can be faxed or sent electronically).

Second, a resignation letter helps determine whether the resignation is effective. Please understand: Just because you have resigned, that does not mean that the resignation is effective. The effectiveness of a resignation depends on a number of differing and varied factors. Is there a contract term that defines when a resignation is effective? Are there payment protocols that dictate when the "last money" is received and, therefore, when the resignation has become effective? Does the company handbook say anything about resigning? Are you in a company where some type of mandated exit interview marks the moment of an effective resignation? Delivering the resignation letter thus at minimum puts you in a position to literally determine whether there are any challenges or preconditions concerning the effectiveness of the resignation.

The next purpose served by a letter of resignation is to control what you say when you resign. People who write letters such as the one written by Don *speak that way when they resign.* We will address in a moment what you, when resigning, should and should not say; however, unquestionably, someone who delivers a long and emotional letter—"good" emotions or "bad" emotions—will not be able to contain himself when resigning. Resigning in person is hard. People get nervous and upset and feel elated and guilty, all at once. If you are in that frame of mind, you will give up the ship, as they say, in a variety of ways that serve no good purpose for you or the hiring company. Some people make false promises about what they will and will not do at the next company ("I have no intention of going after my direct reports," when of course they do). Others give the equivalent of an exit interview in which they criticize everything from the coffee in the kitchen to the CEO's decision to hire the new manager to whom they are now resigning. Some departing employees feel it is incumbent upon them to profess their undying gratification and appreciation for "everything you and the company did for me," and believe that such gushing will make the situation somehow better. *A short, well written resignation letter reminds you, in the moment, to be quiet and be precise and, most of all, to be brief.*

Absent unusual circumstances, here is what a letter of resignation (for people who are leaving alone, without contractual or other legal resignation restrictions) should typically look like:

Dear [Supervisor's Name]:

I hereby resign. I am joining [Next Company]. My new address is ___, and I can be reached at [New Company Telephone Number]. If anyone asks for me, please give them this information.

My office key is in my desk drawer, along with my building pass. All of my files are located outside my office, in the cabinets to the right of the office door. As a courtesy, I left my personal belongings in my office, and will make arrangements to pick them up some time next week.

Yours very truly,

Candidate

Can you spot all of the things that such a properly worded resignation letter accomplishes? (Go back and try, really, before reading the next paragraph).

First, believe it or not, it lets the employer know that neither you nor the hiring company is afraid. How so? Let me start the answer to that question by asking a question: During the Transitioning process, when a candidate is given a draft of the resignation letter in the type of form just shown above and told to use it, what do you think is the number one, number one by far, initial question asked by the candidate? In almost every single instance, the candidate will ask, in words or substance, "Do I have to tell them where I am going?" The answer is always "Yes," but for reasons you might not imagine. We disclose the next place of employment for the following reasons: There is no reason to hide that fact since nothing wrong is being done; if that fact is hidden, it looks like the move is somehow improper, or that there has been pre-resignation wrongdoing; the very first question you will be asked by the manager when resigning is "where are you going," and we of course do not want you lying; and, by definition, you are resigning to join a competitor, so the manager will know, literally or figuratively, in a matter of minutes the name of the new company. So, why be afraid to make that disclosure up front?

A focused resignation letter also sends a signal to the Old Company manager, even before you speak, that you are well prepared to resign and that, therefore, the manager is unlikely to get much information, or for that matter a rise, out of you. In other words, the form letter you just read is a professionally constructed letter and Old Company will know it, and that alone sends a purposeful message. Employees who are not well trained before they resign write letters like the one Don slipped under his boss's door. Any manager worth his or her salt who receives a Don Jenkins-like letter will recognize that the employee sitting in front of them is ripe for handling. Consequently, submitting a professional resignation letter, before any words are spoken, immediately sets the tone and parameters of the resignation.

Short, properly written resignation letters also protect against the possibility of the manager ratcheting things up right out of the gate. Most managers got to where they are because they are good at what they do and because they are aggressive enough to climb to a leadership position. Part of enjoying a supervisory position is getting to tell others what to do and, as you rise through the ranks, having fewer folks controlling your actions. Resignations, for an instant, switch the controls; for a moment, it is the employee, not the supervisor, who sets the agenda and, instinctively, managers will not react well to that loss of control. Therefore, keep things short and quiet and calm. Don's letter, if it were given to me, would make me want to go right after Don even before he started to speak.

Finally, a well written resignation letter memorializes the fact that you, properly, left everything behind, including even your personal effects, and that the company was asked to cooperate in the transition. Making a record of what you did not remove, and how professionally you behaved, is very important.

Now, can you count the ways Don's resignation letter is wrong? How many examples did you come up with in total? Make a list before you read on to see how close you came.

I spot twelve:

"I have really enjoyed my time at Smolthouse." Really? In the letter, you bash the company. Don't be disingenuous or, for that matter, patronizing.

"I've learned a lot from everyone, especially you[.]" Translation: The company taught me everything I know and now I am delivering that knowledge to its top competitor.

"I am moving on to a new challenge[.]" Read by Don's manager's boss, this will sound like, "you, Ms. Line Manager, failed to appreciate that Don, a rising star, needed more opportunity to grow at Smolthouse and you are therefore the reason for the company's resultant lost revenue."

"My resignation has nothing to do with the way I have been treated[.]" Ok, so when Smolthouse sues Don, and Don wants to explain that the real reason he left was because of all the ways he was mistreated, the resignation letter will become Exhibit A.

"It really meant a lot to me when you helped put together the party for my birthday and I will always remember the flowers you sent after my grandmother passed away." First, this is not group hug time. Don is leaving, and leaving in a way that will hurt both Smolthouse and the manager. Such euphemisms will not ease those emotions. Second, now you've made the manager feel like an idiot for doing all those nice things.

"That being said, I am worried about the direction that Smolthouse is heading." How many years has Don been in the party planning business? Five? After five years, he thinks he has the ability to tell one of the largest party planning operations in the country in what "direction" they should be going?

"I worked really hard on the strategy committee[.]" This is what is known, in legal terms, as an "admission." Put in lay terms, Don has just admitted that, because he was on the strategy committee, he was privy to not only some of the company's most confidential information but, still worse, it is confidential information about future business plans. Oh, and by the way, he learned that highly confidential information while planning his departure and, now, he's going to take that information to a direct competitor. The quoted sentence will be Paragraph No. 1 in Smolthouse's lawsuit.

"If Smolthouse continues…it will drive many of its talented planners to join competitors." Great, now the situation is not just about Don, alone, wanting to leave. Now it is, potentially, a multi-person departure problem. Will that make Smolthouse less, or more, aggressive in its response to Don's departure?

"…Smolthouse is headed straight for an iceberg[.]" Besides being overly dramatic and unfounded, if Smolthouse believes that Don has, or will, speak to others in that manner, it will have no choice but to take legal action to prove him wrong and to stop him from voicing such reputational slander.

"...I hope to remain friends with many of the people I have met here." This is what Smolthouse will hear: "At my new company, which competes with Smolthouse, I will stay in touch with my peers at Smolthouse so they know how wonderful things are at the competition."

"Good luck in the future[.]" The manager will think: You left me on the Titanic to join the iceberg that did the damage to us and you wish me good luck?

"...keep in touch." Why, because there might also be a spot for the manager at Next Company?

Twelve bad things said in just a one-page letter, and Don and his manager have not yet even spoken.

Please know also that I have seen resignation letters that were far worse than what Don wrote.

4.   What To Say When You Resign

In addition to a well-written letter of resignation, when you finally do speak with your manager, you need to be prepared for the conversation.

In almost every instance, nothing good—only bad—can happen when a recruit goes into his manager's office to resign. Typically, nothing you can say will, for example, dissuade the now-former company from taking steps to prevent the business losses—or employee departures—that may follow your resignation. Regardless of what words you use, the manager will still be personally upset and know that there will be a direct and negative economic fallout for the company generally, and for her specifically. Please believe me when I say that nothing can change the fact that you are leaving, that you will be trying to divert revenue and perhaps key personnel to your new company, that other employees and companies will soon know of your departure (and, therefore, of the company's vulnerability to defections), and that all of this raises a serious question about how well the company and the manager handle rising stars. Spare me also how "great" your relationship is with the company generally and your manager specifically. *Be quiet when resigning.*

I think the act of resigning should take less than three minutes. Look at your watch, right now, for three minutes. Three minutes is a long time.

I know that resigning should not take more than three minutes because the resignation dance, if you will, can be highly predictable if well-choreographed. It is initiated, of course, by your knock on the manager's door, followed by you asking if you can come in for a moment. Five seconds. You then walk into the office and sit down across the desk. Unless the office is huge, or a chair needs to be moved into place, or the manager is on the phone, only another five seconds or so, at most, passes. You then summon the nerve to utter those all-important words, "I am resigning." At that moment, a total of fifteen seconds or so has passed and, now, the real clock starts.

The manager, if trained properly, will likely begin to ask all sorts of questions designed to address the upcoming harms. "Do you know you have a contract?" "Have you spoken already to any clients?" "Have you told other employees?" "What will you be doing in your new job?" In my experience, the best way to derail the interrogation—and to stop the clock—is to be armed with a phrase that you can repeat often enough to get your message across; namely, that you are well prepared and that you will not be divulging information. I like, "I've made my decision and I need to go." Say such a phrase two or three times, which typically takes about two minutes to sink in, and the resignation ends. Three minutes.

Chapter 3

I Am Don Jenkins

I was once Don Jenkins. I was a partner in a large and still-terrific law firm, who decided that I wanted to leave my partnership and start what would, ultimately, be a competing enterprise (albeit much smaller). So I know from both a personal and professional perspective what it feels like to plan in secret to leave, and what it feels like to resign in person (to someone I very much respected and still do). I also know how scary and how hard it is to not take steps—in advance of resigning—that will allow you to get a head start. But I was luckier than the Don Jenkins in the case study because I did not need any help to understand how to leave properly, and how to behave after resigning. After all, I helped write the Don Jenkins story.

But what if you are not a legal expert on Transitioning and you are considering leaving your job to join, or create, a competitor? What can you do to better prepare for such a move?

1. Read Up Before Deciding Whether To Resign

First, you got a great start by reading this book. The Dos and Don'ts apply to you, even if no one from the hiring company tells you so. The same is true in terms of how you resign and what your resignation letter should say. Similarly, take to heart how careful you must be about not changing your work habits. Remember to never lie about your Transitioning. In other words, by reading this book, an individual considering a move is already substantially better positioned to ensure a successful transition and to mitigate risk.

Another benefit of reading this book is that it will help give you, the person who may be going, a better feel, before you engage with potential new companies, of whether you can move successfully. Why? Because if, in your heart of hearts, you believe, for example, that, in order to succeed at New Company you must pre-solicit revenue sources or pre-recruit subordinates, and you must, for example, remove original records, then maybe you are not really in a position at the time to make such a move. Transitioning to a competitor is a hard process; doing it correctly and having people follow is even harder. So be honest with yourself before taking that first exploratory step: "If I behave the way Manchel is saying I should behave, will I end up at New Company with the ability to succeed at that firm?"

The third benefit for an individual imparted by what is contained in this book is that it allows you to take an important measure of the hiring company. I speak almost every day to people who are leaving, or considering leaving, their jobs. Of the people with whom I speak, almost all of them are leaving to join a competitor. My view, my strong view, is that, if the company doing the hiring does not adhere to the protocols outlined in Part Two of this book, and if it does not provide you with experienced legal guidance on how to transition over, that is a poor reflection on the company you are considering. *Every single person who leaves to join a competitor must understand that the process is fraught with risks, business and legal.* This is even truer should you, the candidate, have an existing employment agreement with post-employment restrictions. Many companies still ignore the pitfalls of lateral hiring, but they do so at their, and your, peril.

2.   Why Are You Leaving And Will You Succeed?

Be honest with yourself. If you are leaving for the money, own it. If you want to go because you were overlooked for a promotion you thought you deserved, admit that to yourself and be brutally honest about whether you actually should have received the promotion. If you think New Company will provide you with a better, kinder, more welcoming environment, just exactly how do you know such things? What makes you think the next place is "more

entrepreneurial," and do you even really know what that means—
to be entrepreneurial—in a corporate setting? Are you just stuck in
a rut, or bored and, if so, is a move likely to solve the malaise? A
word to the wise: You might be able to kid the recruiters, but don't
fool yourself. Unless you take genuine stock of what is making you
consider a move, you are bound to end up on the losing end.

Similarly, if you believe that employees and/or revenue sources
need to follow you to the next company for you to succeed there,
then take stock about how many truly need to move (hint: it is not
all of them) and what they need to hear from you, post-resigning
of course, in order to make the move. Note that I said, "take stock."
What I did not say is speak to them, or take a survey.

Here is an evaluation exercise I like to use. Imagine there are
three corn silos (and I have no idea why I use that imagery, maybe it's the Vermonter in me). In the first silo are the names of the
people you are certain will follow you once they know where you
have landed. In the second silo are the names of those folks who,
with relatively little, shall we say, nudging, will very likely join
you. In the third silo are individuals who, realistically, will need to
be pitched, or convinced, that the right move is to stick with you.
Be sure you are honest and conservative about your category selections.
Then, ask yourself the following question: Can you make out a successful business plan for yourself at Next Company based on just
the names in the first silo? If not, how many people do you think
you might need to join you from the second silo? Warning: If you
need too many people from the second silo, or if you need anyone
from the third silo in order to do well at Next Company, the resulting answer is almost always to stay put.

3. Sorry, But You Need A Lawyer, Now

Having done both a personal and a business assessment, you con-
cluded that it is possible to successfully transition out of your current company. What's next? Do you need a lawyer to help you with
that process? The answer is yes, but not just any lawyer.

Generally, you need to look for what are called "employment
lawyers." These are attorneys who concentrate their practices on
employee-driven issues. For example, although they are wonder-

ful at drafting wills, I would not hire an attorney who specializes in Trust & Estate work to help me with Transitioning. Also, I am skeptical (in this context) of attorneys who are generalists when it comes to Transitioning. To be clear, many general practitioners make for wonderful counsel, and are certainly quite capable of, say, reviewing an employment agreement. However (sticking with my obsession with farm imagery), what separates the wheat from the chaff in my world is not whether an attorney can read an employment contract; rather, I want an attorney who, because of targeted and extensive experience, can read the employment agreement and give solid advice about the attendant tea leaves. As I hope you can appreciate by now, it is the blending of law and business that leads to successful Transitioning. In my firm, we act as counsel to multiple Transitioning employees each week. That is the level of experience for which you should be looking.

So, you decide to make the smart move and to speak with an experienced attorney about the potential transition. What exactly is the attorney supposed to do, and how much should it cost? In terms of work, if you have a contract, make sure the attorney reviews the contract. That being said, I don't appreciate lawyers who simply read back the words in an agreement. At this point in her life, my mother, who is in the camping business, could probably give decent advice on the terms a contract contains. What is really needed is a sense of what impact the terms, or the absence of terms, has on whether a competitor is likely to want to hire you, and on your ability to have people, be they employees or revenue sources, follow you.

The next question for your counsel will typically be whether, and if so, when, to discuss the existence of the contract with the hiring company. This is a very delicate issue that is greatly influenced by three things: The law of the state(s) in which negotiations are occurring; the language of the contract itself (*e.g.*, some contracts require disclosure to the hiring company and other agreements prohibit the revealing of contract terms); and the temperament, if you will, of the hiring company. As a general rule, I favor giving a copy of the contract to the hiring firm. Why? Because everyone should know where they stand. The last thing you want is to be hired and then have your new company receive a (surprise) letter demanding, pursuant to a contract about which New Company has no knowledge, that you stop working or that you cease contacting revenue sources and former employees. In many instances, the result of such a corporate surprise might be termination.

Your attorney also has to be able to guide you on the Dos and Don'ts as they apply to you under the applicable state law. Remember: The pre-departure Rules laid out in this book are general guidelines. Moving the needle from general to specific requires the advice of a lawyer who is highly experienced in this field. To give you an idea of how specialized my Transitioning work is: I am not a general employment lawyer (*e.g.,* I do not handle discrimination issues); I do not negotiate compensation, ever; and I do not draft employment contracts. *All I do is make sure that Transitioning employees come over the right way, and with the least amount of risk or exposure.* Oh, and by the way, if the attorney you chose truly knows what he or she is doing (absent special circumstances such as an incredibly lengthy and complicated agreement), getting you from reading the contract to helping you resign should take about an hour, maybe ninety minutes.

One last observation: When you organize yourself in these ways before speaking with a potential new employer, you already look better to hiring companies. In my experience, hiring companies are very impressed when a candidate, on his own, takes it upon himself to fully appreciate and prepare for the challenges inherent in Transitioning. It shows professionalism, initiative, and maturity. Look at Don: If you were the manager of the company that hired him, and you had read this book before meeting Don, what would you think of Don's behavior? More importantly, would you want him to be one of your employees? Few things look better to a hiring company than people who, on their own, handle themselves well.

Congratulations! You made it successfully to the resignation! But there is still more work for you to do, so read on. "Why?" you may ask. "The next part is all about how companies should manage the hiring process, why is that of any relevance to me?" Good question. Remember what was discussed at the very outset of this book: You are not Transitioning alone. By definition there are (at least) two partners in the Transitioning process: You and the hiring company. If the hiring company is not as prepared as you, if it is not well versed in the Dos and Don'ts, then it is putting you (and itself) at risk. Think about what happened when Don was asked what clients would follow him. Had Don read this book, he would have known that the hiring company was not well-versed in the fundamental Rules of Transitioning. In other words, by reading Part Two of this book, you can be in a position to assess the companies with which you are talking on their ability to ensure that your Transitioning goes smoothly.

PART TWO

HOW COMPANIES BEST MANAGE THE PROCESS OF HIRING FROM THE COMPETITION

It's now time for some of you to put your corporate hiring hat back on. Armed with an understanding of how a candidate is supposed to behave before joining your company, you will ideally appreciate the importance, and the process, described in the following pages, of implementing and maintaining an effective Transitioning Program.

Chapter 4

Why Companies Need A Transitioning Program And How To Implement It

Hiring, let alone hiring from a competitor, should not be done haphazardly, or as a one-off type of operation. I hope readers can see already that Transitioning from the competition is fraught with pitfalls and risks. Bad corporate recruiting techniques also lead to at least two other unwanted results: There are fewer recruits, and the recruits, as new employees, are less likely to succeed. Consequently, there are at least four reasons (I do like the rule of four) for a Transitioning Program: To help protect against risks—economic, legal and business; to make the company's recruiters better at recruiting; to make the company present, to outside candidates, as more professional and better organized; and to identify and hire better recruits (who, in turn, will be so pleased with the process that they will promote the company to their peers).

As is the case with most significant corporate initiatives, for any such Program to succeed there must be buy-in at the top of the company, which is not always easy. The difficulty lies typically in the numbers. On one hand, companies that are about to hire, say, the president of a competing company, understand that, as part of the process, there will be Transitioning costs, including legal. But at the other end of the business spectrum is the company that typically hires lower-level lateral employees, or smaller companies that worry about being big enough to afford having a formal process in place before anyone starts at their new job. Another factor is how most companies have viewed hiring for a long time: Attracting, interviewing, and onboarding. So what is this thing you call a "Transitioning Program?" Consequently, by proposing the implementation of a Transitioning Program, I am raising up front cost issues and also asking people to change embedded hiring practices. Additionally, most companies view lawyers as a drain on resources and as naysayers, and as only being harbingers of negativity and expense and litigation. It is difficult to convince corporate executives that, in the context of hiring, a good lawyer can actually be a revenue generator. Regardless, the point is that what all well-run businesses share in common, in my experience, is a watchful eye on expenses; therefore, I am regularly asked why money should be spent on a Transitioning Program.

The short answer is that you either spend it up front or spend multiples of the investment later. Seriously, if a company is committed as part of its business plan to drive revenue or management growth in any way by hiring from the competition, it will either invest relatively little now in a Transitioning Program, or a lot later on in a lawsuit. These days, between the applicable law and difficult-to-achieve-business goals, and the shrinking of industries and the scarcity of available revenue sources, *every single hire from the competition comes with the potential for litigation*. Once again, it's in the numbers: If a business is in the practice of hiring laterally, a recruit and the company will almost certainly someday be sued, especially if the Transitioning is not done properly. Listen up, it's how I make my living: If a Transitioning Program is implemented properly and run efficiently, the cost of the legal work associated with that program should be dramatically less than what the company will pay in damages and litigation fees or settlement for just one recruit who comes over the wrong way. The longer business answer is that, in my experience, a properly run Transitioning Program generates more hires because it leads to better-trained people recruiting better recruits in a better way.

One more point on the topic of litigation risk. The specter of litigation should not dissuade a company from hiring good employees from the competition or scare individuals away from moving. Under the right Transitioning Program, people transition correctly and lawfully. Does that mean there is then no risk of litigation? Unfortunately, it does not. Okay, so then why have a Transitioning Program? Because, while I cannot stop a company from suing over the loss of a key employee, I can make sure that, if there is litigation, the recruit and the hiring company have the best chance of winning. The first time Old Company spends a boatload of money on litigation and loses (because the recruit left the correct way), it will think long and hard about filing that second lawsuit. I'll say it again for those of you not following closely: It's in the numbers. If done properly, what is spent on the Transitioning Program should never approach what will be lost on just one transition that goes sideways. For me, those are the only pertinent economics.

The way to actually implement a Transitioning Program is to first train the folks at the company who will ultimately be responsible for Transitioning candidates (*e.g.* the head of Human Resources, or the owner of a small company who directly handles hiring) and, then, to train the people who report to them. I will be hated by many a lawyer after I utter the following words, but so be it: *We do not charge our clients either for the initial Transitioning training, or for follow-up sessions devoted to refreshing former trainees or training new recruiting staff.* All we ask is that our travel expenses are reimbursed and that we be hired to participate in the subsequent recruiting efforts. The reason I don't charge for Transitioning Program training is because, literally, I am willing to put my money where my mouth is: If a company lets me train those involved in recruiting, the company will recruit more, and it is in connection with the actual recruiting that I will make my money. Also, by partnering with companies, I move from being viewed as a drag on resources to being seen as a revenue generator. As noted, a lawyer's fundamental job in a Transitioning Program is to deliver sound legal advice in a way that actually drives revenue and hiring, and not to act simply as a siphoning-off of resources.

One more point before we start. I understand completely the fear companies and individuals have sometimes about involving a lawyer in purely business efforts, especially in the hiring process; a fear that includes concerns ranging from cost to the fallout that can occur if a lawyer starts spouting "legalese" to an already-nervous recruit. Consequently, to succeed in the recruiting world, effective legal support must be technically correct, economically worthwhile, and delivered in such a way that the candidate is not frightened off. Never in my years of practice has someone not gone forward with the transition because they were turned off or frightened by my involvement. In fact, the opposite is true: Without exception, every client and every recruit has viewed my participation in the Transitioning process as an asset. To a business, my corporate clients *market* the Transitioning Program outlined in Part Two of this book. Frankly, in this day and age, it is almost impossible to find any experienced and conscientious employee who does not need and want professional legal guidance in connection with a job move.

So now, Mr. or Ms. CEO, since it's free, can we start the training? I usually get a "yes" answer to that question....

1.   Transitioning Training Starts At The Top And Always Stays Exactly The Same

As noted, effective Transitioning Program training starts at the top and works its way down to those who recruit for the company. My definition of "those who recruit for the company" is actually quite expansive. On one end of the spectrum are the obvious recruiters, such as paid headhunters and HR Personnel. But what I have learned over the years is that, by design or default, there are many, many others at a company who typically play a meaningful role in recruiting; *e.g.*, managers who spend time over coffee with potential hires, peers who regularly introduce lateral candidates to the company, dog-and-pony teams set up to meet with targeted employees, in-house transition assistance groups. It is therefore incumbent upon the company to determine, first, who needs to be trained as part of a Transitioning Program. Since the training is free, and the advice being rendered is about sticking to sound business and ethical practices, the company might as well be overly inclusive.

Once the company determines the potential universe of trainees, the training needs to be delivered from top to bottom in a perfectly uniform manner. When I say perfectly uniform, I mean just that: Anyone in my firm who provides Transitioning training uses the exact same language, the exact same words, with every trainee, regardless of whether we are working with the company's CEO or standing in front of a group of two hundred people. Can you guess why there is such a focus on the exactness of the language? Let me answer the question with a question: If you are the head of HR, the person ultimately responsible for every hire, and you hear from a line manager that a recruit stated that the lawyer (and it is always the lawyer who is blamed), "said he could tell the Best Man at his wedding about us before resigning," how would you know whether the recruit was telling the truth? How would you know that the lawyer did not actually tell the candidate to go pre-solicit the Best Man? The only way for you to know whether anyone actually gave the candidate permission to pre-solicit his Best Man (which would not happen since it is a violation of Rule One), is if you are certain about exactly what every recruit is being told. Consequently, from the highest-level executive participating in hiring, to every person and group thereafter, and every single time the process is rolled further out, *the exact same instructions and directives will be given, using the exact same words.* If any recruit ever says that she was told something besides what was recited at the training session, it sends a signal that the recruit, at best, misheard.

That sameness, the rigid consistency of the communications presented in a well-structured Transitioning Program thus provides another valuable screening benefit: It weeds out candidates who, once hired, might not make the best employees. Think about it. What company wants to hire someone who refuses to follow just four (important) Rules? If the recruit does not follow the Dos and Don'ts or, worse yet, says they are adhering to those Rules but is lying, the company knows before making the hire the type of employee the candidate will be and, in most instances, that candidate will therefore not be hired. This added layer of assessment is thus a valuable side benefit of the exactness of a good Transitioning Program.

The next step in implementing the Transitioning Program is therefore teaching company recruiters the Dos and Don'ts. (See? I *told* you to read Part One of this book!) It doesn't matter how good folks already are at recruiting, or how eager they are to bring over additional lateral hires; if they do not understand and deliver the substantive message the company wants presented to candidates, all the same risks remain. A Transitioning Program is only as good as its weakest link, and I want senior-level people to be able to immediately spot such a link and fix it. So I take a very simple approach to training folks on the Dos and Don'ts: Whether it is one person, or a hundred managers in an auditorium, I take the person

I am about to train (or a representative from the audience) through the Rules and teach them the stages of Transitioning, as if they were an actual recruit. In other words, rather than lecture, we role-play. I have the obvious role, that of the attorney assigned to assist in the Transitioning, and my "volunteer" plays the role of the recruit who has progressed to the point where the company believes she should be introduced into the Transitioning Program. From there, from the moment I first pick up the phone to say hello to the recruit (a substantial amount of our work is done via telephone and not in person), through completing my talk, I use the same words, in the same order with my hypothetical candidate. As such, everyone watching knows exactly what is being said to each and every candidate.

2.   Good Transitioning Programs Vet Candidates Early On In The Hiring Process

The next part of a Transitioning Program rollout is convincing the corporate trainees that every potential hire needs an early, stand-alone on-boarding risk assessment.

A good Transitioning Program attorney ought to be able to tell the company what possible risks and costs exist for each potential hire well before the lateral prospect even rises to the level of a "real" candidate. Does the employee have an existing employment agreement? If so, risks increase. Does that agreement contain a non-compete, a non-solicit and/or a confidentiality clause? If so, risks increase. Are they currently employed by a company that is litigious? If so, risks increase. Do they work in a pro-enforcement state, or do they live, for example, in California where, by statute, non-competition agreements are unenforceable? Is the potential candidate home grown, or did her current company hire her laterally? Did the recruit develop his revenue sources by going, literally or figuratively, door to door, or were those sources given to him by the company when a senior employee retired? Did the executive candidate sign his employment agreement in connection with the sale of a business he founded? Is the recruit's current employer experiencing larger than normal turnover? Is the current company in play? Will this candidate take the hiring company into a new business arena or, conversely, take away the only such resource the competitor has in that area? A successful Transitioning Program has someone in place with enough experience to read such tea leaves (and there are many more "leaves").

In order to vet candidates properly and successfully, the company recruiters also need to be trained in procedure.

A well-run Transitioning Program is actually made up of multiple, discrete, formalized parts. Initially, people need to be trained on the importance of timing. In other words, while it is wonderful if a manager knows the Dos and Don'ts, and that she is fully committed to making sure all of her recruits follow those Rules, what good is her dedication if the recruit is first introduced to the process the day before he resigns? I can provide the single greatest legal advice on why a recruit should not pre-solicit or take original records, but if the company sends them my way the day before they resign, the odds are overwhelming that the company and I are too late; it is about to hire a Don Jenkins and the bad deeds have already been done. Honestly, I know very, very few businesspeople planning a move on their own who, without guidance, would naturally act in strict accordance with all of the Rules. Thus, late recruit deliveries typically put a company in the worst of all worlds: It has spent money on a Transitioning Program, but that Program has now been rendered useless, and the company is about to hire someone who will be putting the company (and the hire) at real risk just because the timing was off. For these reasons, in terms of timing, companies should, except in the rarest of circumstances, place the lateral hire into the Transitioning Program pipeline at least a month before the planned resignation date.

3. Good Transitioning Programs Monitor Communications

The next procedural piece of a Transitioning Program concerns communications. First, no company should allow its recruiters or candidates to call the outside Transitioning Program attorneys directly. When a recruiter determines that a candidate is viable, and that the hiring process has progressed beyond attracting and interviewing to Transitioning, there should be one person (at the most two) at the company whom the recruiter calls: Someone whose role is to act as the corporate Transitioning Program gatekeeper. Establishing a designated corporate gatekeeper ensures two things. One, it controls legal costs: Law firms bill time only on candidates who have been properly screened by the gatekeeper for the next hiring phase. It is wasteful and costly and inefficient to be giving out legal advice to someone who is not going to actually transfer. (Sorry, but line recruiters always think they have a greater potential success for a hire than actually exists.) Next, having a corporate gatekeeper ensures that the recruiter has built in sufficient time; namely, if the gatekeeper is called the day before the candidate is going to resign, the recruiter will be told, typically, "too late." The gatekeeper's role thus needs to be established formally.

Who plays the gatekeeper role in any given business depends in large measure on the size of the hiring company and the volume of lateral hiring. So, for example, in large, multi-state companies, there is often a head of recruiting. In smaller operations, the head of Human Resources plays the role of gatekeeper. In still smaller businesses, it is not unusual to see the CEO or CFO deciding when the time is right for Transitioning to begin. What all size operations share in common, though, is this: Choose one person, who is well trained in the Dos and Don'ts and on how to resign, and who understands the importance of timing.

It may sound somewhat trivial, but perfecting the scheduling of the candidate's initial Dos and Don'ts call is actually very important.

There are different views on who should advise the recruit on the Dos and Don'ts. I recommend it be handled by an attorney, for two reasons. First, although presented in gentle terms, the issues being addressed by our four fundamental Transition Rules are legal in nature and, therefore, substantively, it is legal, not business advice being rendered; a task best left to a lawyer. (Also, as noted, the law of each state will have to be considered and applied.) Second, when the lawyer advises the potential hire on how to transition, those instructions, in almost all instances, are privileged and may not be revealed, even in litigation. However, if the Rules were imparted by a company employee, that communication would arguably not be privileged and, therefore, the company may have just turned a key corporate recruiter into a key litigation witness.

But I digress. Let's get back to how to properly arrange the Dos and Don'ts call. Here is my overriding advice in terms of how to schedule the initial call: Don't force the recruit to play phone tag. Take a step back. We all have busy schedules. Compounding that complication, however, is the fact that the candidate is trying to coordinate things on her end in secret and without tipping off her employer. Additionally, you are now telling the recruit she is going to be speaking with a lawyer. Hiring companies generally, and Transitioning Programs specifically, must be sensitive to these factors because it's always the little things that candidates remember. For this reason, I recommend the following procedure.

When the time comes for the recruit to go through the Dos and Don'ts, a call that typically takes no more than 45 minutes or so, the corporate gatekeeper (or the gatekeeper's subordinate) should reach out for legal counsel and ask for at least three one-hour slots (even though the call itself typically takes about 45 minutes, build in some extra time) when the lawyer is available to go over the Rules. The time slots offered by the attorney should all be for early morning, lunch time, or late afternoon; times when it would be normal for the candidate not to be in the office (Rule Three). Second, the gatekeeper (of course using the recruit's personal e-mail only) should then e-mail the recruit and have that person choose one of the slots. Third, the gatekeeper should then confirm the time with both the lawyer and the candidate and give the recruit the lawyer's number to call. Finally, the recruit, not the person giving the advice, calls at the appointed time. Sounds trivial, but I cannot overstate how failing to efficiently arrange what is ultimately such a simple introduction negatively impacts the overall performance of a Transitioning Program.

Here's a free piece of advice (even though I hope you paid for the book): I *never* make the initial call to a recruit. *Never.* I don't like the optics or risks of such a call. I don't want to ever leave a message, and I never know if I am going to catch the recruit in a bad moment (*e.g.*, with his manager standing outside the door). Remember: I deal almost exclusively with people who are leaving their jobs, so the company, if it ever learns I called, would know something is happening. (Once, a recruit decided to play my message on his cellphone speaker. Bad move.) Also, of course, I would never schedule a call to be taken at a candidate's office.

4.   Transitioning Program Language

I call the earliest part of a Transitioning Program "No Man's Land." Everyone from the potential hire to the recruiter who is involved in the recruitment process is kind of "in between" everything, making communications and decisions fuzzy at best. In my experience, the early part of Transitioning presents the greatest challenges in any recruiting effort, and also generates the greatest recruiting legal risks. Why? Because everyone involved is on the surface talking all lovey dovey (sorry for the fancy legal lingo), but at the moment they are actually all working on their own agenda. In practical terms, it comes down to this: The hiring company wants information sufficient to be convinced that the recruit will make an excellent executive or a terrific producer (or employee), and the candidate needs to impress the company in part with information he reveals in order to get the job and the desired compensation package. It's the perfect litigation storm. To spice things up even more, most likely, none of the ongoing conversations are privileged.

This fundamental tension is caused by the fact that recruits cannot reveal confidential information about their current employer to the hiring company, but the hiring company needs information about the recruit. What is "confidential" depends on a myriad of factors, such as the law of the state in which the recruit lives (and, perhaps, where the company resides), potentially applicable contract terms, handbook provisions, Trade Secret Statutes, etc. Typically, and this truly varies by state and by industry, a recruit can talk about himself, and what he has accomplished. But when does "my stuff" and "my personal story" cross the line into revealing corporate confidential information? (Sorry, the answer is, "It depends.")

Please do not think that you will read here—or that you have already read—the definitive "answer" to what can and cannot be discussed while Transitioning. It is not possible to create an exhaustive list, let alone one that stands up under the laws of every state, of what information may properly be exchanged during this early phase of the hiring process. Generally, when it comes to the question of what information may lawfully be disclosed, staying broad is always better than being specific. Take, for example, the recruiting of a manager. In my experience, most courts (or arbitrators) are not troubled by a manager describing how she built her unit, in terms of employees and sales, or by telling the potential hiring company the types of clients served and products sold by her unit or her market focus. But where the line is often crossed is when the manager, for example, names particular employees that she believes can be brought over, or discloses the financial incentives it would take to get the subordinates to move.

Don't shake your head in feigned disgust. "No one would do such things," you mutter to yourself while reading. "Manchel is just making this stuff up so we hire him." Understandable feelings, but untrue points. I'm telling you, without advance guidance, without a solid Transitioning Program, not only will recruits reveal confidential information, the hiring company's recruiters *will encourage them to do so.*

How did Don do during his stint in No Man's Land? Actually, not too badly. Go back and re-read the paragraphs about his interview with Bud Fox. Note that, while the questions asked of Don were pointed, his responses were general:

Q: "First, if we offered you the MD position, would you bring any of your clients with you?"

A. "I am sure that they would continue to demand my services. In fact, I was just speaking yesterday with one of my clients [and] he was asking when I was going to leave[.]"

So, Don gets close to but does not cross the line. He speaks confidently, and generally, about "his clients" and "a client," but does not reveal any names, and does not suggest in his response that the clients were pre-solicited. (He took the same approach when asked about employees who might follow him.)

5. Beware The "Wrinkles"

Just because the Transitioning has been planned wonderfully does not always mean all will go smoothly. The reason, of course, is the fact that all your planning is, by definition, only on *your* side. However, when the candidate actually steps into the room to resign, he by definition brings the *other* side directly into the equation; a fact that always creates instant variables. For that reason, a successful

Transitioning Program has top situational solvers available on that proverbial Friday afternoon.

The people chosen to handle any fallout from the resignation must be calm problem solvers. Indeed, rather than call them "problems," which is a term that makes recruits nervous, I instruct folks to call the issues that inevitably pop up during a resignation "wrinkles." Again, it's not (really) semantics. Think about it: If someone on your team tells you in a calm voice that "there are a couple of wrinkles to handle," as opposed to announcing that "we have a problem on our hands," who sounds more in control and less worried? It is mission-critical that no matter what wrinkles arise, overall calmness prevails. When situations come up, everyone from the recruit to the recruiter to the recruit's soon-to-be new boss will already be on edge. But there is nothing to worry about because we have a Transitioning Program! If the setup is correct, the right people will be in the right place and they will have the skills to calmly and quickly resolve the issue. When they do, the Program shines! I actually call one of my favorite corporate recruiters "The Wrinkle Man" precisely because he is such a terrific on-the-spot solver.

Be prepared for all sorts of stuff. What happens if the manager is not in her office when the recruit goes to resign? What if she is in the office, but won't meet with the hire? What if she says, "I don't accept your resignation"? What if she says, "You cannot resign to me, you have to resign to Julie"? What if she says that the employee has to stay long enough to give an exit interview? What if she says that the employee must give two weeks' notice, and stay, because that is what the contract provides? What if she says that the employee has to immediately clean out his office (which would mess up plans to head straight over to his new company)? What if there is no one in the office to whom the employee can resign? What if the manager claims that money is owed by the employee and that, until the money is paid back, the notice of resignation is not effective? What if the manager just won't answer the knock on the door (true story)? You get the point: Lots of things can happen along the way, and an effective Transitioning Program will have people in place who can handle such contingencies calmly and in real time.

Chapter 5

Now What?

First, I will tell you what not to do once the recruit resigns: Do not pop champagne and celebrate; do not start bragging around the office and around town; do not issue a fancy press release (unless that is part of a considered strategy); do not let the recruit start barraging revenue sources or direct reports with sales pitches and hiring outreaches; and do not issue an internal announcement filled with gratuitous hyperbole to company employees. Come on Steve, why not? We won! Let's get—so sorry for the pun—the party started!

For the company, the Transitioning process is actually not quite over yet. A low-key corporate approach at this moment is critical because the hiring business needs to understand that it is being scrutinized by a number of very important audiences at the time of the hiring. Specifically, four significant groups are watching and reacting: The former company; revenue sources and direct reports; competitors; and New Company's own employees. For different reasons, the emotions of each of these groups are running high, so it is important that a relatively quiet approach be taken initially. Said another way, we are trying to put the Sleeping Giants back to sleep, not get them more worked up!

The fundamental point of this chapter is thus that a well-constructed Transitioning Program does not end at the moment of the hire. A successful transition ends only after the employee is positioned to recreate his prior successes at New Company; this can occur only after any issues with the former company are resolved, after the New Company's existing employees come to see the benefits of the new hire, and after competitors realize that the arrival of the lateral hire will not help them pry loose employees from the hiring company.

1.   Communicating Post-Resignation To Revenue Sources And (Former) Subordinates

It is a business fact of life that people who join the competition, in almost every instance, can succeed in their new company only by convincing revenue sources (or subordinates, in the case of executives and managers) to switch firms along with them. Indeed, this is typically a big part of the reason why the lateral employee was hired: To transfer new revenue and/or new people into the hiring company. It is an equally unavoidable fact that the now-former company will likely do what it can to stop revenue and additional employees from leaving. Appreciating the simultaneous presence of these polar opposite forces must color the hiring company's short-term conduct and temperament.

Don't kid yourself, the former firm will find out exactly what the new hire is up to. How? One hundred percent of the time, I repeat, one hundred percent of the time, one or more of the people contacted by the new hire about her new company will also be contacted by the former company. If the hiring company assumes otherwise, or allows the hire to assume and therefore act otherwise, the risks of litigation increase materially. Think about it: If both sides of the hire are contacting revenue sources and subordinates, it means that one or more of those sources or subordinates is repeating to the now-former company what the new hire is saying. Nothing, and I really do mean nothing, incenses a company that is already on the losing side of a hire more than hearing that its former employee is aggressively pitching his new company or badmouthing his former place of employment. Consequently, the first step, post-hiring, is to train the hire on how to properly speak to revenue sources (and former colleagues) after he resigns.

I believe strongly that, when a hire joins a new company, regardless of whether he had an employment agreement, he should not pitch clients (or subordinates) in a heavy-handed way. As a threshold matter, those people have a choice of whether to stay or follow, and no one likes to be harangued about moving. Additionally, as noted, since these people are also going to be contacted by the former company, I want the message they repeat to be that the new company is competing fairly by simply letting folks know that they have the right to choose where to do business, or to work, at either the old or the new company. Moreover, overly aggressive solicitations, in my view, send the wrong message about the new company: How bad can it be over there that the recruit needs to work so hard to get us to join him? Finally, a lateral employee who needs to hit his revenue sources hard, just like the CEO who needs to hammer on former direct reports, always makes me question whether, in fact, the targets of such efforts really are loyal. For all these reasons, I suggest that a very gentle, low-key approach be made during the initial outreach. Oh, and then there is that contractual non-solicitation or non-recruit clause you need to handle.

A word as well about new hires who bad-mouth their former firm when first communicating about the move: Don't. In actuality, I have come across very, very few lateral hires who truly say bad things to others about their former employer. The far more typical situation is that the hire does not appreciate that all the nice things she is saying about her new company necessarily reflect poorly on the old company and, therefore, her "positive" commentary will be viewed most unfavorably by the prior firm. You see folks, at the moment of a new hiring, it is a zero-sum game. For example, if the recruit says, nicely, that he joined the new company because he thinks it has great technology, he is by definition saying that his former firm's technology was lacking. Similarly, when a just-departed hire tells a center of influence that he left because he loves the direction of the new place, he is saying, without question, that where he left was heading downhill. Just remember, it's all relative, and not in a good sense.

There is something else going on at the former company: An angry manager is watching.

To some, the following might be a startling revelation: Managers have feelings. They get hurt. They feel joy and pain. They bleed when cut. Okay, perhaps a bit dramatic, but you would be shocked at how most employees, and plenty of upper-level managers, fail to account for the human side of managing generally, let alone at the time of resigning. They also fail to appreciate that managers come with all sorts of temperaments, backgrounds, world views, business experience (or relative lack thereof) and personalities. It is therefore a mistake to end one's analysis of how to behave simply by thinking just about the former company as opposed to about the former manager. Managers are definitely not one size fits all, and only a sensitive, low-key approach will help settle things down.

But what if the former boss is the candidate's friend? Surely he won't do anything bad after she resigns, right? Here are some simple truths about the "friend": The recruit decided to leave; the two now have competing interests; and one or both of them will get hurt further if those interests are clouded because of a friendship. The hire's interest is to make a successful transition out of the company to a competitor. The success of that transition, by definition, means harm to the corporation for which she worked and, specifically, to the former boss. Again, everyone is in a zero-sum game. One "friend" left and, as part of that transition, she will inevitably take revenue sources or employees to New Company. At that very same moment, and I believe this is true as regards every jurisdiction in which I have been involved in recruiting, the other "friend," the manager, has the legal (and oftentimes contractual) duty to try to stop all that from happening. Consequently, if the candidate tells her "friend" about their plans or thoughts, then at best she puts the manager in a very difficult position: Do they honor the friendship and keep what is said in confidence, or do they honor their duty to the company and reveal what was disclosed in order to stop any further corporate damage? Here is some really sophisticated legal advice: When it comes to reaching back to speak with a former supervisor, keep the recruit's mouth shut. If the boss really is a friend, the best way to protect him is to not involve him; and, if he really is a friend, the friendship will survive the transition.

2. New Co-Workers

The hiring company's employees, in particular those who consider themselves peers of the new hire, as well as anyone who thought he should have gotten the new hire's job, at best will be jealous about the new guy. Lower-level employees will be nervous about the new guy. At worst, all three sets of employees will become the company's Don Jenkins: Employees who feel overlooked, under-appreciated, at risk, disenfranchised and capable of transitioning their skills and business to a competitor. So watch out. Unless the hiring company stays focused on its current employees when the new hire comes across, current employees will not like the attention and support and (perceived) money that is being showered upon the recruit. Rest assured, I have seen such things as office space location, the size of the desk a recruit was given, the proverbial shiny new BMW, and the constant visits and glad-handing, drive other employees right into the arms of a competitor. A line must therefore be drawn between welcoming the hired lateral, and unduly promoting the new employee.

3. Watch Your Competitors As They Are Watching You

Lastly, while keeping a low profile, watch competitors closely. Few things cause the competition to focus their recruiting efforts on a company more than the belief that a significant new hire will shake up the company that she is joining. I am not the only person who knows that newcomers, especially high-level newcomers, cause what I call corporate agitation. Corporate agitation, in turn, generates employees questioning things that might not have been questioned before. Everyone knows that the new senior vice president is "likely to make changes," or has a "style of her own." They "know" additionally that the company is backing the new approach; in fact, that is why she was hired. Ask any recruiter and they will tell you the same: The best chance of prying someone away from where they work is to get in touch with a person who is already thinking about whether they should stay. Honestly, in my overall experience, it is pretty rare that, once someone starts to explore departing, he ends up not going. For the employee who feels overlooked, the grass really is greener on the other side. Remember, a lateral hire often generates targeted recruiting attention.

Unfortunately, there is no magic answer to the question of "How long do we need to act in this low-key way?" I have seen a former company file a lawsuit in two business days, and I have defended lawsuits filed as long as a year after the candidate resigned. For these reasons, I always approach the question from a business perspective when asked whether it is now okay to "turn on the jets." What is it, precisely, that is not being achieved using the gentle and low-key approach with revenue sources and employees and the competition? If the answer is just, "We want more faster," then my follow-up is to ask what everyone is willing to risk. Can they live with being sued? Can they withstand employees leaving? What impact, even if employees do not leave, will there be just because recruiters and headhunters are targeting firm personnel? Remember people, choices have consequences, so choose wisely lest you get what you deserve.

Congratulations! The company attracted a wonderful candidate, the company's recruiters placed the recruit in the Transitioning Program pipeline at just the right moment, the lateral employee adhered strictly to the Dos and Don'ts and resigned the right way and, now, he is out and over and acting just as instructed. We are done.

Conclusion

As I hope can be appreciated, everyone has a little Don Jenkins in them when it comes to job Transitioning. Frankly, in my almost thirty years of experience, I have seen relatively few people *intentionally* act badly when joining a competitor. Most of those who violate the law, or a contract, do so because they were not taught the lessons contained in this book, and did not know what the hiring company should and should not do, or how to properly retain legal counsel. Unfortunately, a lack of knowledge on how to move correctly is not a defense when sued. So don't be too hard on Don Jenkins, but try not to *be* Don Jenkins.

It is equally certain that the risks—both business and legal—are real, as also are the emotions that come with job Transitioning. Be sensitive to all those factors. Whether drafting your letter of resignation or interviewing with Next Company, stay alert and keep your focus on the rules and methods and processes discussed in the chapters you read. And remember the stories, too, as they serve a singular purpose: Bad behavior leads to bad results. It also shines an unflattering spotlight.

I hope you are convinced as well that, moving forward, writings about job Transitioning should not be "either for the individual or for the company but not for both." It sounds so trite, but it is nevertheless true: The employee who leaves his or her company is *joining* another, competing company. Consequently, unless those two moving pieces are in sync, either or both could be the downfall of the overall process. Think about it: You do everything correctly, but the hiring company wrongfully gets you to give it confidential information; alternatively, the company has a wonderful Transitioning Program in place, but the recruit refuses to follow the Rules. Result: Costly litigation. Will the sum of the two parts of Transitioning be positive, neutral or negative?

I hope this book taught some other important lessons. First, there is no excuse for not hiring, or for not preparing and resigning, well. Proper Transitioning is both teachable and learnable. For heaven's sake, there are only four Rules that make up the Dos and Don'ts. It's not that hard to keep from being a Don Jenkins and, while no lateral move is typically ever perfectly executed, running a recruit through a Transitioning Program goes a long way toward mitigating and managing risk.

Second, in the final analysis, all this may not seem like rocket science, but it takes discipline among all the participants. Think about how many people touch upon the hiring process, from those involved in the attracting, to the people who handle interviewing, to personnel managing the (new) Transitioning Program, to those responsible for onboarding. Anyone along that chain who steps out of line puts the whole hire at risk. You are, as the saying goes, only as strong as the weakest link.

I hope, too, that the benefits of the approach I advocate are appreciated. People who transition better create less risk. Recruits willing to follow ethical and meaningful directives make for better employees; conversely, the candidate who won't follow good business advice or, worse yet, says he is but fails to do so, will not make a good employee. As for those involved in the Transitioning Program, the holistic approach I champion will almost certainly make for better recruiters who will do more recruiting. At the same time, corporate executives, because of the exactness of the Program, will have an effective way of monitoring those who participate. Last, but not least, everyone working together materially reduces the risk of damages from potentially resulting lawsuits.

To reap the full benefits of this book, go back now and reread the case study. Come on, spare me, it's only eight pages! What I believe you will take away is how much of Transitioning concerns not just the legal issues presented when hiring from the competition, but also the psychology of that process. Training recruiters and recruits on the Dos and Don'ts is relatively straightforward. Convincing a nervous candidate, and the recruiter managing the hiring process, that the employee should not run to his new BMW after slipping his resignation under the door of a boss who is at that moment attending her son's birthday party, and all that comes in between and after, is the hard part. Bottom line: One cannot take a strictly legal approach to the task of Transitioning, but one also cannot avoid the impact the law has on that process. Marrying those two concepts is mission-critical, and it is the singular focus of my professional life work.

Let me therefore end on a personal note. My father taught at the University of Vermont for almost fifty years. His discipline was film, movies. Note my use of the term "discipline." No one thought that discipline could be brought to the study of movies; what you brought to movies was popcorn and soda. In fact, in order to teach his discipline, my father had to write his own textbook because at the time no expert literature on the subject existed. If my father can turn watching movies into a rigorous discipline, so too can his son when it comes to job Transitioning. Let's just hope this apple did not fall too far from the tree.

Okay. It's 2:00 on Friday.
Knock, knock.
Happy Transitioning.

9 781733 040846